ParkerRodriguez

Planning
Urban Design
Landscape Architecture

101 N. Union Street
Suite 320
Alexandria, VA 22314

Michael Kasiske | Thies Schröder

Gartenkunst 2001
Garden Art 2001

Potsdam Bundesgartenschau
Potsdam National Horticultural Show

Birkhäuser - Verlag für Architektur
Birkhäuser - Publishers for Architecture
Basel · Berlin · Boston

Dieses Buch entstand mit freundlicher Unterstützung der Bundesgartenschau Potsdam 2001 GmbH und der Entwicklungsträger Bornstedter
Feld GmbH.

This book was kindly supported by Bundesgartenschau Potsdam 2001
GmbH and Entwicklungsträger Bornstedter Feld GmbH.

Übersetzung | Translation: Michael Robinson, London
Übersetzung Essay Peter Wilson ins Deutsche | Translation essay
Peter Wilson into German: Annette Wiethüchter, Berlin

Layout und Umschlaggestaltung | Layout and cover design:
buero kleinschmidt, Berlin

Druck | Printing: Medialis, Berlin
Lithographie | Lithography: Licht & Tiefe, Berlin

A CIP catalogue record for this book is available from the Library of
Congress, Washington, D.C., USA

Die Deutsche Bibliothek – CIP-Einheitsaufnahme

Gartenkunst 2001 : Potsdam, Bundesgartenschau = Garden art 2001 /
Michael Kasiske / Thies Schröder. [Übers.: Michael Robinson]. – Basel ;
Boston ; Berlin : Birkhäuser, 2001
  ISBN 3-7643-6531-5

© 2001 Birkhäuser - Publishers for Architecture,
P.O.Box 133, CH-4010 Basel, Switzerland
A member of the BertelsmannSpringer Publishing Group
Printed on acid-free paper produced from chlorine-free pulp. TCF ∞
Printed in Germany
ISBN 3-7643-6531-5

9 8 7 6 5 4 3 2 1   www.birkhauser.ch

INHALT

CONTENTS

Wiedergewinnung des öffentlichen Raums

15 und 4 lauten zwei magische Zahlen der Potsdamer Bundesgartenschau. 15 BUGA-Projekte in 4 Kulissen, Parks, Gärten, Plätze, Ufer, eine große Halle und weitere kleine Anlagen wurden seit 1996 vorbereitet. Potsdam, eine eher kleinere Großstadt mit großer baukünstlerischer Tradition und einem reichen Weltkulturerbe, hat einen weiten Schritt nach vorn geschafft – architektonisch hinein in das 21. Jahrhundert, ohne den Bezug zu seiner Baugeschichte aus den Augen zu verlieren.

Potsdam, trotz beachtlicher Leistungen in der Stadterneuerung in den neunziger Jahren häufig unglücklich, ja verzweifelt über seine bauliche Entwicklung, dabei stets Halt und Identität im baulichen Erbe des 18. und 19. Jahrhunderts suchend, entdeckt 2001 sein Selbstbewußtsein als moderne Stadt wieder. Potsdam feiert 170 BUGA-Tage lang die Wiedergewinnung des öffentlichen Raums.

Stadtentwicklung gehört zu den vornehmsten Aufgaben einer demokratischen Gesellschaft. Geht es doch um die Gestaltung unserer Lebensräume – konkret und vor Ort, funktional, sozial, ökologisch, baukünstlerisch, ästhetisch... nachhaltig. Die Demokratie als Bauherr – ohne ein umfassendes Engagement der öffentlichen Hand bleibt sie ein leeres Wort. Doch angesichts ihrer massiven Verarmung auf kommunaler Ebene droht ein Rückzug der verfaßten Stadtgesellschaft aus öffentlichen Aufgaben. Selten gelingt es, aus der Not eine Tugend zu machen und öffentliches Engagement privat zu kompensieren.

Wie keine andere Stadt in den neuen Bundesländern hat Potsdam bereits früh die Weichen zur Bewahrung seiner Handlungsfähigkeit in der Stadtentwicklung gestellt. Sanierungs- und Entwicklungsgebiete wurden beschlossen, mit dem Bornstedter Feld ein großes Militärgebiet als Konversionsprojekt geschultert. Und für das Jahr 2001 wurde ein Ziel gesetzt: die Realisierung eines ehrgeizigen Entwicklungsprogramms für den städtischen Freiraum.

Der BUGA-Termin half dabei wie eine Lokomotive. Mehr als je zuvor bei einer Bundesgartenschau dienen in Potsdam alle Vorhaben der Stadtentwicklung, vor allem der neue Volkspark im Bornstedter Feld. Mit der Qualität seiner architektonischen Gestaltung, seinem spannenden Raumgefüge, seinen Kontrasten, der Vielseitigkeit seines Spiel- und Sportangebots und nicht zuletzt seinen Kunstobjekten wird er eine herausragende Stellung in der Region Berlin-Potsdam einnehmen.

Der neue Park schließt eine weiträumige Lücke in einem nunmehr wundervoll wahrnehmbaren Spannungs- und Bilderbogen, der durch mehr als zwei Jahrhunderte Gartenkunst in Potsdam führt: vom Babelsberger Park über Glienicke, die Glienicker Brücke, den Neuen Garten und den Pfingstberg hinüber zum Ruinenberg, zu Schloß und Park Sanssouci. Eine einzigartige Einladung an alle Liebhaber niveauvoller Gartenkunst.

Das Bornstedter Feld hat in kürzester Zeit sein Gesicht dramatisch gewandelt. Potsdams Antlitz ist in dieser Zeit noch schöner geworden. Der weitere Weg ist damit – hoffentlich – vorgezeichnet. Wenn dies ausstrahlen, andere Städte ermutigen sollte, um so besser.

Volker Härtig ist Geschäftsführer der Entwicklungsträger Bornstedter Feld GmbH.

Vorwort von **Jochen Sandner**

Landschaft als Zeitschicht

Potsdam ist ein Inbegriff zeitgenössischer Landschaftsarchitektur – seit nunmehr drei Jahrhunderten.

Mit dem Park im Bornstedter Feld konnten wir ein neues, aktuelles Stück Potsdamer Landschaftsarchitektur realisieren. Auch in anderen Bereichen der Stadt ist es gelungen, Zeichen zu setzen. Mit dem Platz der Einheit entstand eine moderne Gestaltsprache auf historischem Grund. Das Projekt zur Wiederentdeckung des Stadtkanals wurde begonnen. Der Lustgarten, einst Teil des Schloßensembles, erstrahlt in neuer Form. Die Freundschaftsinsel ist wieder das, was Karl Foerster und der Bornimer Kreis einst in ihr sahen.

Doch die Bundesgartenschau 2001 in Potsdam ist mehr als aktive Stadt- und Freiraumentwicklung. Nicht nur Lenné kommt – so in der rekonstruierten, von ihm gestalteten Feldflur – zu neuen Ehren. Noch wichtiger ist mir, daß es den Landschaftsarchitekten der Gegenwart durchaus im Wissen um die Leistungen Lennés und in Kenntnis der historischen Potsdamer Kulturlandschaft gelang, dieser einmaligen Landschaft eine neue Zeitschicht hinzuzufügen.

Nicht mehr ein Landschaftsarchitekt hat dies alles erdacht, sondern viele Teams traten an, mußten koordiniert werden. Ein gutes Werk der Gegenwart ist meist das Werk vieler. Probleme inbegriffen.

In Potsdam sind die Inhalte und Ziele zeitgenössischer Landschaftsarchitektur begriffen worden. Der Park im Bornstedter Feld ist viel beachteter Ausdruck dieser neuen Qualitäten. Denn er ist schön und funktional zugleich. Er ist für eine aktive Freizeit konzipiert, und für stilles Genießen. Er hat so zahlreiche Facetten, wie die berühmten Potsdamer Sichtfächer Blicke anbieten. Und fällt dennoch nicht auseinander. Waldpark und Wiesenpark, Remisenpark und Wälle – das alles ist so vielfältig wie für ein anregendes Parkerlebnis notwendig. Doch die BUGA hat mehr erreicht. Die Investitionen in die Stadtentwicklung entsprechen dem Achtfachen der eigentlichen BUGA-Mittel. Überall in der Stadt sind die Veränderungen sichtbar.

Potsdam mußte nicht neu erfunden, kann nun aber neu gesehen werden. Die Landschaftsarchitektur der Gegenwart hat hier Zeichen gesetzt.

Jochen Sandner ist Geschäftsführer der Bundesgartenschau (BUGA) Potsdam 2001 GmbH.

Regaining public space

15 and 4 are two magic numbers for the National Horticultural Show in Potsdam. There are 15 show projects in 4 settings, parks, gardens, squares and riverside; a large hall and other small complexes have been in preparation since 1996. Potsdam, essentially a small metropolis with a great architectural tradition and a rich World Heritage, is now taking a major step forward – moving architecturally into the 21st century, without losing its connections with its historical architectural past.

Despite considerable urban renewal achievements in the nineties, the city has often been unhappy, indeed in despair about its architectural development. It has always looked for a foothold and a sense of identity in the architectural legacy of the 18th and 19th centuries, and in 2001 it has regained its self-confidence as a modern city. For the 170 days of the National Horticultural Show Potsdam is celebrating the fact that it has regained its public space.

Urban development is one of the primary duties of a democratic society. We have to work on creating the spaces in which we live constantly – concretely and on the spot, functionally, socially, ecologically, architecturally, aesthetically ... sustainable. Democracy builds – without wide-ranging commitment from the public purse, it remains an empty word. But given a massive tightening of the public purse-strings at local level, we are threatened with withdrawal of the constitutional urban society from public tasks. It is rare to make a virtue of necessity and to compensate privately for a lack of public commitment.

Like no other town in the former East Germany, Potsdam made it clear at an early stage that it intended to retain its powers to act in terms of urban development. Areas were identified for refurbishment and redevelopment, and a large military area was taken on board as a conversion project in the form of the Bornstedter Feld. And a target was set for the year 2001: realizing an ambitious development programme for open urban spaces.

The date for the Show gave tremendous impetus. More than ever before, every project associated with it will help urban development, above all the new people's park in the Bornstedter Feld. The quality of its architectural design, its exciting spatial structure, its contrasts, the varied range of play and sports facilities it offers and not least its art objects will give it an outstanding position in the Berlin-Potsdam region.

The new park closes a wide gap in an arc of excitement and images that spans over two hundred years of garden art in Potsdam: from the Babelsberg Park via Glienicke, the Glienicke Bridge, the Neuer Garten and the Pfingstberg, then on to the Ruinenberg, to the palace and park of Sanssouci. A unique invitation to all lovers of high-quality garden art.

The Bornstedter Feld has changed its looks dramatically in the shortest possible time. Potsdam has acquired an even more beautiful face in this period. We hope that this will give clear pointers to the road ahead. And if this all serves to encourage other towns, so much the better.

Volker Härtig is managing director of Entwicklungsträger Bornstedter Feld GmbH.

Foreword by **Jochen Sandner**

Landscape as a layer of time

Potsdam is the epitome of contemporary landscape architecture – and has been for three centuries.

We have been able to realize a new, up-to-date piece of Potsdam landscape architecture in the form of the Park in the Bornstedter Feld. And considerable impact has been made in other parts of the town as well. Unity Square demonstrates a contemporary design language on a historical site. A start has been made on the project for rediscovering the municipal canal. The Lustgarten, once part of the Schloss ensemble, is now resplendent in its new glory. Friendship Island is restored to the form in which Karl Foerster and the Bornim circle once saw it.

But the 2001 National Horticultural Show in Potsdam is more than active development of the town and its open spaces. Lenné is not the only person to bask in new glory – in the reconstructed meadowland that he designed, for example. It is even more important to me that contemporary landscape architects were able to add a new layer of time to this unique landscape, in full awareness of the Lenné's achievements and in full knowledge of Potsdam's historical parkland and gardens.

It was no longer a single landscape architect who devised all these projects, but many teams took part and had to be co-ordinated. Good contemporary work is usually the work of many people. Problems included.

The significance and aims of contemporary landscape architecture have been fully grasped in Potsdam. The Park in the Bornstedter Feld is a highly esteemed expression of these new qualities. It is beautiful and functional at the same time. It is conceived for active leisure, and to be enjoyed quietly. It has as many facets as the famous Potsdam fanned views. And yet it still holds together. Wooded Park and Meadow Park, the Shelter Park and the ramparts – all this is as varied as a stimulating park experience needs to be. But the National Horticultural Show has achieved even more. The urban development investments represent more than eight times the actual resources available for the Show. Changes are visible all over the town.

Potsdam did not need to be reinvented, but it can now be seen in a new light. Contemporary landscape architecture has set an outstanding example here.

Jochen Sandner is managing director of Bundesgartenschau (BUGA) Potsdam 2001 GmbH.

Gartenkunst
zwischen gestern und morgen

Als landschaftliches Gesamtkunstwerk, als Stadt der Schlösser und Gärten, wurde Potsdam berühmt. Dieser Berühmtheit hat sich die Residenzstadt in ihrer Geschichte immer, wenn auch mit unterschiedlicher Intensität, gewidmet. Das Potsdam der Zukunft wird eine Stadt der Gartenkunst bleiben, freilich nicht als romantische Idylle der Monarchen, sondern als gestalteter öffentlicher Raum.

In den neunziger Jahren des letzten Jahrhunderts stellte sich Potsdam einer europaweiten Tendenz, im öffentlichen Raum den Schwerpunkt der Stadtentwicklung zu sehen. Barcelona oder Lyon mit ihren historischen Stadtkernen, aber auch moderne Städte wie Rotterdam wurden durch die Neuformulierung ihres öffentlichen Raumes zu Leitbildern für die Potsdamer Stadtentwicklung. Immer ging und geht es allerdings zugleich um die Wiedergewinnung des historischen Stadtgrundrisses.

Die Diskussion um die Notwendigkeit neuer Plätze und Parks für Potsdam, und zwar nutzbarer Parks, nicht repräsentativer Schmuckgrünanlagen, begann umgehend nach dem Ende der DDR. Arbeitsgruppen aus Studierenden, freien Planern, Verwaltungsmitarbeitern und Politikern schlossen sich zusammen, um den genius loci Potsdams neu zu definieren. Dabei traten Rekonstruktion und Reformulierung des Stadtraumes teils einander skeptisch entgegen, teils als strategische Partner nebeneinander an. Die nachholende Modernisierung war wie überall auch mit nachholender Kritik am modernen Städtebau und Wiederaufbau verknüpft. Die offene Frage lautete: Welche zurückliegende Phase der Stadt- und Landschaftsentwicklung ist verpflichtende Referenz für zukünftige Entwicklungen?

Nun ist Potsdam seit langem nicht mehr Residenzstadt, und seit kaum einem Jahrzehnt auch nicht mehr aktive Militärstadt. Die Konversion seit Jahrhunderten militärisch genutzter Flächen bot in Potsdam die Chance, städtische Räume für neue, für zivile Nutzungen zu öffnen. Skizzen zum zukünftigen Umriß der Stadt wurden produziert und publiziert und die besondere Beachtung des öffentlichen Raumes als Grundgerüst des Typus der europäischen Stadt empfohlen. So entstand die Idee, Städtebau und Landschaftsentwicklung zu koppeln. Das Bornstedter Feld wurde als Stadterweiterungsgebiet entdeckt, und zugleich wuchs der Plan, mittels einer Bundesgartenschau neue Freiräume zu gewinnen. Konkrete Planungen und Wettbewerbe, so für das Bornstedter Feld im Norden der Stadt, für den Platz der

Einheit, für den Alten Markt und den Lustgarten im historischen Zentrum sowie für die Wasserlagen Potsdams wurden auf den Weg gebracht und bis 2001 überwiegend umgesetzt.

Es sind die vielfältigen Qualitäten der „Insel Potsdam", die Besucher und Bewohner der Stadt wie der Kulturlandschaft – untrennbar ineinander verwoben – faszinieren. Zum Gartenkunstwerk verbinden sich Landschaften und Parkgestaltungen mit städtebaulichen und architektonischen Elementen wie dem abgerissenen barocken Stadtschloß (1660) mit seinem inzwischen im Wiederaufbau befindlichen Fortunaportal (1701) oder dem Rokoko-Schloß Sanssouci (1745–1747) von Georg Wenzeslaus von Knobelsdorff aus der Regierungszeit Friedrichs des Großen. Dagegen hat das 20. Jahrhundert in Potsdam nur wenige beachtenswerte Spuren hinterlassen, darunter die Freundschaftsinsel des Bornimer Kreises um Karl Foerster und der expressionistische Einsteinturm (1917-1921) des Architekten Erich Mendelsohn. Ansonsten ist die Zeit seit dem Zweiten Weltkrieg für Potsdam eine der Verluste an Bausubstanz und an Geschichtsspuren gewesen. Heute ist besonders die Unvollständigkeit der Potsdamer Silhouette eine faszinierende Herausforderung. Wie kann an die reiche Bau- und Gartenkunsttradition einer Stadt in landschaftlich äußerst reizvoller Umgebung, die jedoch nicht mehr als geschlossenes Ensemble vorliegt, angeknüpft werden? In Potsdam werden beide Wege ausprobiert: die zeitgenössische Fortschreibung und Ergänzung sowie die Rückgewinnung des Verlorenen. Beide Ansätze sind umstritten, jedoch nur auf den ersten Blick nicht vereinbar.

Es sind die bekannten Regeln der Gartenkunst wie des Städtebaus, die heutige Gestaltung definieren helfen. Es sind die Regeln der Komposition, der Komposition von Bauten wie von Blütenfarben oder von Herbstlaub der Bäume in ausgewählter, stimmiger Vielfalt, wie sie im Park Sanssouci einst so vorbildlich gelungen ist. Oder die Verbindung der Dimensionen Weite, Dichte und Nähe in einem Park, in einer Stadt. Es sind spannungsreiche Wegeführungen und eine Anlage geschickt akzentuierende Wasserspiegelungen, die einen Ort ansehnlich machen, ihm einen Geist verleihen. Seit dem 19. Jahrhundert, als Peter Joseph Lenné schrieb, das Landschaftsbild gewinne erst „durch seine Beziehung auf den Menschen ... seine Vollendung", hat sich an diesen

Prinzipien wenig geändert. „Wie mächtig die Natur in ihren Urformen auf unser Gemüth wirken und wie viel uns davon in der Landschaft übrig geblieben sein mag, immer wird die Spur des menschlichen Daseins einen erfreulichen Zusatz zu den aufgeregten Empfindungen und Gedanken darbieten. Je mehr die Gestalt der Landschaft von der Urform abweicht und der Kultur angehört, desto inniger müssen die Beziehungen der kunstgerechten Formen zu den Wohnstellen und desto kräftiger diese, als Zentralpunkte des Ganzen, herausgehoben werden." (Peter Joseph Lenné als Mitautor von Bethe: „Über Trift- und Feldpflanzungen", 1826)

Und dennoch sind Landschaftsarchitektur und Städtebau heute so vieles mehr, müssen es sein: ideenreiche und attraktive Nutzungsangebote in der Konkurrenz der Freizeitgesellschaft müssen die Abbildung eines gesellschaftlichen Ideals in der Kulturlandschaft zumindest ergänzen – oft genug verdecken sie die Idee auch. Die Ordnung der Natur allein darzustellen genügt nicht; die Idee der Natur mit ihren gesellschaftswissenschaftlichen, ethisch-moralischen und philosophischen Anklängen soll nun nicht mehr nur im landschaftlichen Ideal, sondern auch im städtischen Park für sich selbst zum Ausdruck kommen. Romantische Wildheit ist heute ebenso Motiv des zeitgemäßen Parks wie die flexibel nutzbare Wiese. Wo einst repräsentatives Grün weltliche Macht und später aufklärerische Intention in der Gestaltung von Plätzen, Parks und Gärten verband, kommt heute demokratische Teilhabe zum Ausdruck.

Der Stadtplatz wie der Volkspark stehen aber nicht nur allen offen, sie sollen auch allen gefallen. Während ehemals der König in den Entwurf eingriff, wird heute zur Pressekonferenz geladen, eine Ausstellung eröffnet, der Bürger zur Beteiligung aufgefordert und unentwegt die Baustelle vorab besichtigt. Transparenz lautet das Motto, und allgegenwärtig ist deshalb die Meinung, die sich Bürger wie Experten schon lange vor seiner Eröffnung, kaum daß die ersten Bäume gepflanzt, der erste Rasen eingesät ist, von einem Park gemacht haben. Um so überzeugender muß ein Park ab seinem frühesten Jugendstadium wirken. Die Baumschulen haben sich europaweit als Anbieter von Großbäumen auf den Wunsch nach einer sofort fertigen Kulisse eingestellt. Landschaftsarchitektur wie Architektur müssen in kürzester Zeit fertige Produkte präsentieren.

Was bei der Gestaltung eines Stadtplatzes noch gelingen mag, nämlich nach Abschluß der Baumaßnahme einen fertigen Ort zur Inbesitznahme anzubieten, fällt bei der Gestaltung eines Parks oder Gartens, bei jeder Aufgabe, die mit dem Baustoff Pflanze arbeitet, sehr viel schwerer. Die Landschaftsarchitekten gehen heute teils von der Überzeugung ab, eine fertig durchdachte Parkkulisse entwerfen zu müssen. Vielmehr geht es darum, Initialmaßnahmen einer Entwicklung vorzusehen. Der Landschaftspark Duisburg-Nord,

entworfen vom Büro Latz + Partner, setzt auf ehemaligen Industrieflächen und Verkehrsanlagen auf ein Konzept der sukzessiven Aneignung. Über Jahre schreibt Latz seine Planungen analog zu den konkreten Entwicklungen vor Ort fort. Und setzt mit der Zeit immer neue Akzente, die sich zu einem Bild in permanenter Veränderung, ständiger Steigerung der Dichte der Eindrücke entwickeln: erst die Sicherung und landschaftsgestalterische Betonung ehemaliger Hochöfen, dann die Gestaltung der Eingangsbereiche, inzwischen die Gärten in ehemaligen Kohlebunkern und die Sport- und Spielangebote im ehemaligen Klärbecken sowie an den hohen Betonkletterwänden, aktuell ein neuer Wasserkreislauf und in Zukunft die vorsichtige Erschließung der großen Sukzessionsfläche auf ehemaligem Bahngelände für die Besucher.

Noch stärker als Latz für seinen Park Duisburg-Nord betont das niederländische Landschaftsarchitekturbüro West 8 die Bedeutung der Initiierung von Prozessen des Wachsens und Veränderns. Ihr Entwurf für die Außenanlagen des Amsterdamer Flughafen Schiphol ist bestimmt von Pflanzaktionen, die bewußt ein fertiges Bild vermeiden. Allerorten setzten die Landschaftsarchitekten junge Birken, darunter säten sie Klee. Stehen die Bäume neuen Verkehrsstrassen oder Baumaßnahmen im Weg, werden sie eben wieder ausgepflanzt. West 8 initiieren Prozesse, halten aber nicht an einem einmal gefaßten Bild fest.

Das Initiieren von Prozessen wird inzwischen für so wesentlich gehalten, daß es auch in die Ästhetik eines Parkentwurfs eingreift. Zum einen ermöglicht diese Entwurfsstrategie einen Umgang mit der Pflanze, die Entwicklung zuläßt, nicht festschreibt, zum anderen haben die Landschaftsarchitekten in Europa ihre Schlüsse aus der in den achtziger Jahren vorherrschenden Betonung der Ökologie gezogen.

Allerdings hat die Prozeßorientierung in der Landschaftsarchitektur die Produktorientierung nicht ablösen können. Die Kritik an der ökologischen Planung war im wesentlichen von der Lust am Gestalten motiviert, am Bilderschaffen. Die besondere Herausforderung liegt heute in der Verknüpfung beider Ansätze, nämlich in der Kunst, den Stadien eines Prozesses attraktive Bilder zuzuordnen. Der Park ist initiierter, auch gesteuerter Prozeß, Navigationshilfe ästhetischen Bewußtseins gegen gestalterische Beliebigkeit.

Daß dennoch eine Offenheit bleibt, nämlich das Vergnügen an der eigenständigen Entwicklung bewußt einkalkulierter und aktiver Aneignung eines Platzes oder Parks durch die Nutzer, zeigt besonders der Schouwburgplein in Rotterdam. Dieser von West 8 gestaltete Theaterplatz ist der attraktivste Platz Europas aus der Gegenwart: eine Bühne für alle mit Requisiten, die zur Inbesitznahme einladen und so permanent neue Bilder produzieren helfen.

Es ist aber nicht genug damit, daß die Stadtlandschaft allen offensteht und allen gefällt. Stadt und Park sollen zugleich animieren zu aktiver Freizeitgestaltung, sollen der Jugend wie dem Alter einen Ort geben, dennoch nur wenige Spuren der Nutzungen tragen. Denn jeder Raum dient auch dem erbaulichen Genießen, dem ruhigen Spaziergang, der weiterhin als Inbegriff gesunder Erholung in den meisten Köpfen Priorität genießt.

Dies alles sind Anforderungen an und zugleich Chancen der Landschaftsarchitektur wie des Städtebaus der Gegenwart. In Form einer offensiven Auseinandersetzung mit der Bedeutung des Städtebaus wie der Gartenkunst gilt es, zeitgemäße Orte und Strukturen zu schaffen, welche der Bewunderung standhalten, die wir in der Potsdamer Kulturlandschaft für Sanssouci oder den Glienicker Park ohne jeden Zweifel aufbringen, während uns an dem Schaffen der Gegenwart immer wieder Zweifel kommen.

Dabei ist die Auseinandersetzung mit der Geschichte, gerade wenn sie – wie in Potsdam – so offen vor aller Augen liegt, kein Selbstzweck, sondern dient der Schulung unseres heutigen Selbst- und Bildverständnisses. Der Katalog der Anforderungen ist keineswegs eine aus der Geschichte vorgegebene Rahmensetzung, sondern in Qualitäten und Quantitäten offen, dennoch nicht beliebig. Die Anforderungen sind differenziert – nach Gruppen der demokratischen Gesellschaft, die es gelernt haben, ihren partikularen Interessen einen gemeinschaftlichen Ausdruck zu verleihen. Nun ist der Anspruch an die aufgelockerte, durchgrünte Stadt, an Parks und Gärten – „wohnungsnahes Grün" heißt es im Gesetzestext – politisch verankert, nicht aber die Art, Gestalt und Funktionsweise dieses Stadtgrüns. Ökologische Entlastung und Regenerationsraum („Ausgleich oder Ersatz für Eingriffe in den Naturhaushalt"), Ruhe und Erholung, Spiel und Sport, weiterhin Licht, Luft und Sonne sind heute allgemein geläufige Ziele einer Planung.

Allerdings ist die Finanzierung und Pflege eines Freiraums aus öffentlichen Mitteln keineswegs mehr eine Selbstverständlichkeit. Stadt- und Landschaftsgestaltung der Gegenwart muß also betriebswirtschaftliche wie volkswirtschaftliche Kalkulationen und Argumentationen kennen und anzuwenden wissen. Sie muß Event-Angebote machen, um auch privatwirtschaftliche Interessen zu mobilisieren, muß Aufmerksamkeit schaffen, möglichst neue Eindrücke vermitteln, die Kultur und Kunst zu ihrem Recht kommen lassen, naturwissenschaftlich unterfütterten Ökobilanzen standhalten,

und über all das die Geschichte der Gartenkunst, der Architektur und des Städtebaus nicht aus den Augen verlieren. Doch die Berücksichtigung aller genannter Faktoren, und vieler weiterer, die sich aus Lage und Umfeld ergeben, bringt selbst noch keinen gelungenen Raum hervor. Das Werk überzeugt erst, wenn es gelingt, einen schönen Ort zu schaffen.

Für Potsdam 2001 gilt die Interdependenz zwischen Geschichte und Gegenwart in besonderer Weise. Deshalb entstand in dieser Stadt in den Jahren der Vorbereitung auf die Bundesgartenschau BUGA 2001, die zugleich Jahre der Suche nach einem zeitgemäßen Park für Potsdam waren, eine spezifische Gelassenheit und eine besondere Anspannung zugleich. Zum einen hat man täglich vor Augen, daß und wie es gelingen kann, schöne Orte zu schaffen, zum anderen ist angesichts dieser in und um Potsdam vielfach belegten, zudem in verschiedenen historischen Epochen nachgewiesenen Tatsache die besondere Verpflichtung offensichtlich: Es mußte gelingen, mit einem neuen Park für Potsdam und einer Vielzahl weiterer Anlagen es den Lennés, Knobelsdorffs, Schinkels, Mendelsohns, Foersters und Matterns vergangener Jahrhunderte gleichzutun, ohne sie zu imitieren. Ziel ist auch heute ein garten- und baukünstlerisches Werk, das in der Gegenwart auf Interesse stößt und in der Zukunft zu den besten Beispielen der Landschaftsarchitektur wie der Architektur gerechnet werden wird.

Das zivile Potsdam, Landeshauptstadt des Bundeslandes Brandenburg zwar, meist aber lediglich als Ausflugsort vor den Toren Berlins wahrgenommen, ist auf der Suche nach neuer Identität und neuer Gestalt zugleich die Stadt der Gärten, Parks und Schlösser geblieben. Als solche wurden große Teile der Potsdamer Stadtlandschaft in den neunziger Jahren zum Weltkulturerbe der UNESCO erklärt. Selbstverständlich gehört diese Entscheidung zu den innerhalb Potsdams ebenso wie im Feuilleton umstrittenen. Immer wieder wurde in kritischer Haltung zu einzelnen Bauprojekten – vom neuen, reichlich banalen Potsdam-Center am Bahnhof bis zum Bau einer Straßenbahntrasse durch die russische Siedlung Alexandrowka zur Erschließung des Stadterweiterungsgebietes Bornstedter Feld – mit der Aberkennung des Welterbe-Status' gedroht. Oder diese Drohung wurde in internen Auseinandersetzungen zumindest vorweggenommen. Aber was ist in Potsdam, dieser bevorzugten und zugleich so empfindlichen, erhebliche Emotionen freisetzenden Stadt, nicht umstritten?

Genau in dieser Situation machte man sich in Potsdam auf, einen Beitrag zu Städtebau und Landschaftsarchitektur der Gegenwart – zur Gartenkunst zwischen gestern und morgen – zu leisten und diesen Beitrag aller Welt anläßlich der BUGA Potsdam 2001 zu präsentieren.

Garden Art between yesterday and tomorrow

Potsdam came to fame as a work of the landscape gardener's art, a town of palaces and parks. And historically it has always worked to cultivate this reputation, though with varying degrees of intensity. The Potsdam of the future will remain a city of the art of gardens: not as the romantic idyll of the monarchs who used to reside here, but as a designed public space.

In the nineties Potsdam addressed a Europe-wide tendency to see open space as the key factor in urban development. Barcelona or Lyon with their historic centres, but also modern cities like Rotterdam, became models for Potsdam's urban development by virtue of the reformulation of their public spaces. Re-establishing the historical town layout always has been and still is an important part of these endeavours.

The discussion about Potsdam's need for new squares and parks, and indeed parks for everyday use, rather than prestigious decorative green spaces, started immediately after the end of the GDR. Students, free-lance planners, administrators and politicians formed working parties to redefine Potsdam's *genius loci*. Within this process, reconstruction and reformulation of the urban space were sometimes critical opponents, and sometimes welcomed each other as strategic partners. Catching up with the modernization process also meant catching up with criticism of modern urban development and reconstruction. The unanswered question was: what past phase of urban and landscape development is the obligatory reference point for future development?

Kings have not lived in Potsdam for a long time now, and it ceased to be an active garrison town just about a decade ago. Converting land that had been used for military purposes for centuries gave Potsdam the opportunity to open up these areas for new, civilian uses. Sketches about the future shape of the town were produced and published, and it was recommended that particular attention should be paid to public space as the basic framework of the European city-type. And so the idea of linking urban and landscape development emerged. The Bornstedter Feld was discovered as an area into which the town could expand, and at the same time the plan grew up of using the National Horticultural Show to gain new open spaces. Concrete planning and competitions, for the Bornstedter Feld in the north of the city, for example, for the Platz der Einheit, for the Alter Markt and the Lustgarten in the historic city centre, and for

Potsdam's riverside were launched, and largely implemented by 2001.

What is so fascinating to visitors and residents of the town about the "Potsdam island" and its park landscape – which are inextricably linked – is that its qualities are so diverse. This work of horticultural art is made up of landscape and park designs with urban and architectural elements like the demolished Baroque Stadtschloss (1660), whose Fortuna Portal (1701) is being rebuilt, or the rococo palace of Sanssouci (1745-1747), designed by Georg Wenzeslaus von Knobelsdorff in the reign of Frederick the Great. Compared with all this, the twentieth century made very little significant impact on Potsdam, but did add the Freundschaftsinsel, designed by Karl Foerster's Bornim circle, and the Expressionist Einstein Tower (1917-1921) by the architect Erich Mendelsohn. Then Potsdam lost building stock and some of the traces left by history in the period after the Second World War. Today the fact that the town's silhouette is so incomplete presents a particularly fascinating challenge. How is it possible to relate to the rich building and horticultural tradition of a town that is surrounded by extremely attractive landscapes but no longer exists as a complete ensemble? Two possible approaches have been tried out in Potsdam: contemporary continuation and completion, or regaining what has been lost. Both approaches are controversial, but only superficially irreconcilable.

The familiar rules of horticulture and urban development help us to define modern design. These are rules affecting composition, composition involving buildings as well as the colour of blossom, or of the trees' autumn foliage in all its carefully chosen and harmonious diversity, a feature exploited very successfully in the park of Sanssouci. Or the combination of dimensions like breadth, density and proximity in a park or in a town. What makes a place look striking and endows it with a spirit of its own is excitingly planned routes, and reflections in water that skilfully accent a group of buildings. Since the 19th century, when Peter Joseph Lenné wrote that a landscape only gained "its perfection ... in relation to man", very little has changed to affect these principles. "However powerfully nature may work on our spirit in her primeval forms, and however much of this may have been left in our landscape, traces of human existence will always offer a pleasing addition to the sensations and thoughts that are triggered. The more the form of the landscape deviates from the primeval form and becomes a part of culture, the more fervently form that does justice to art must relate to the dwelling-places, and the more powerfully they will emphasize this relationship as a central point of the whole." (Peter Joseph Lenné as co-author of Bethe: "Über Trift- und Feldpflanzungen", 1826)

And yet landscape architecture and urban development have become so much more today, which is as it should be: ingenious and attractive uses, competing for people's leisure time, must at least complement the notion of illustrating a social ideal in a landscape developed by man – all too often they conceal that notion. It is not enough to present the order of nature alone; the idea of nature with its sociological, ethical-moral and philosophical echoes should no longer be expressed only in the landscape ideal, but also in the urban park as such. Romantic wildness is as much of a feature of the contemporary park as are grassy areas for flexible use. Once prestigious green expressed secular power, then later enlightened intentions, in the design of squares, parks and gardens, but now it signals democratic participation.

Municipal parks and urban squares are not just open to everyone, they should please everyone as well. The king used to intervene in the design, but now invitations go out to press conferences, exhibitions are opened, the public are invited to participate and people endlessly view the building-site in advance. The key word is transparency, and thus there is a general view about a park held by the man in the street and experts alike well before it opens – in fact even before the first trees have been planted and the first grass sown. And so the park has to be all the more convincing from its first young stages onwards. Tree nurseries all over Europe have now got used to offering mature trees because people want to see an instant backdrop. Both landscape architecture and built architecture have to present completed products in the shortest possible time.

When designing an urban square it might be possible to offer a completed place to be taken over as soon as building is finished, but when designing a park or a garden, or indeed anything involving plants as a building material, it is considerably more difficult. Some of today's landscape architects are moving away from the idea that they have to design a park setting that is completely thought through. They in fact feel that the key is to deal with the initial measures to be taken for a development. The Duisburg-Nord landscape park, designed by Latz + Partner, applies a concept of successive acquisition to former industrial sites and transport facilities. Latz has been continually devising his designs for years, in parallel with the concrete developments on the

spot. And as time passes he constantly sets new directions that develop into an image in a state of permanent change, a continuous increase in the density of the impressions: first he made the former blast furnaces secure and emphasized them within the landscape, then he designed the entrance areas, then came the gardens in former coal bunkers and the sport and play facilities in the former sewage treatment tanks, and he is now working on new ways of circulating water, and in future the large tract of former railway property will be carefully opened up to visitors.

The Dutch landscape architecture practice West 8 emphasize the importance of initiating processes of growth and change even more strongly. Their design for the exterior areas of Amsterdam's Schiphol airport is defined by planting that deliberately avoids creating a finished image. The landscape architects have planted young birches all over the place, and among them they sowed clover. If the trees get in the way of new traffic routes or building work they are simply planted out again. West 8 initiate processes, but do not cling on to any particular image.

Initiating processes is now considered so important that it also impinges on the aesthetics of park design. This design strategy first of all makes it possible to use plants that admit rather than impede development, and it also means that European landscape architects have drawn their conclusions from the emphasis on ecology that was prevalent in the eighties.

However, process orientation in landscape architecture has not been able to replace product orientation completely. Criticism of ecological planning was essentially motivated by enjoyment of creative design, of making pictures. Today the particular challenge lies in linking the two approaches, in other words in the art of allotting attractive images to the stages of a process. The park is both an initiated and a controlled process, a navigation aid for aesthetic awareness as opposed to random design.

The fact that there is still a degree of openness – the fact that pleasure is taken in the independent development of deliberately calculated and active acquisition of a square or park by the users – is particularly well demonstrated by the Schouwburgplein in Rotterdam. The theatre square designed by West 8 is Europe's most attractive contemporary square: a stage for everyone, with properties that tempt you to use them and thus help to create new images all the time.

But it is not enough for the urban landscape to be open and attractive to all. City and park should also provide a stimulus for active use of leisure time, and should be a place for both young and old, and yet carry very few traces of the various uses, as every space is also there for edified enjoyment, and quiet walks, which still have priority in most people's minds as the epitome of healthy recreation.

All these are challenges to and at the same time opportunities for contemporary landscape architects and urban developers. If the significance of urban development and horticulture is to be addressed aggressively, then up-to-date places and structures have to be created that can take their fair share of admiration, of the kind that we find in the Potsdam landscape for Sanssouci or Lenné's Glienicker Park without a shadow of a doubt, while we are still full of doubts about contemporary creations.

But here addressing history, especially if it – as in Potsdam – is so clearly there for all to see, is not an end in itself, but helps to train our contemporary perception of self and images. The catalogue of requirements is by no means a set of restrictions imposed by history, but is open in terms of both quality and quantity, though not random. The requirements are differentiated – according to groups within democratic society who have learned to give their particular interests some sort of communal expression. Now the demand for a townscape that is relieved by green throughout, for parks and gardens – "green spaces in proximity to residential areas" is the legal formulation –, is firmly anchored politically, but the nature, form and the way in which these urban green spaces should function is not. Ecological relief and space for regeneration ("balance or substitute for intervention in natural regulation"), rest and recreation, play and sport, and then light, air and sun as well are general planning aims today.

However, financing and maintaining an open space using public funds cannot be taken for granted any longer. So contemporary urban and landscape design must be aware of and know how to use commercial and general economic calculations and arguments. They must also offer events, so that private financial interests can be mobilized, attract attention, convey the most up-to-date impressions possible that allow culture and art to come into their rights, live up to scientifically backed eco-balances and above all this not lose sight of the history of horticulture, architecture and urban design. But considering all the factors named, and many others that emerge from site and surroundings, does not in itself make a successful space. The work is convincing only if it successfully creates a beautiful space.

Interdependence between history and the present is particularly relevant to the National Horticultural Show 2001. For this reason the years of preparation, which were at the same time years of searching for an up-to-date park for Potsdam, were years of both specific calmness and a special kind of strain. On the one hand people were constantly aware that and how it is possible to create beautiful places, and on the other hand it is obvious that a special obligation is imposed in the face of this fact that has been proved in many

ways and also in many historical periods in and around Potsdam: there was a pressure when creating a new park for Potsdam to do as well as all the Lennés, Knobelsdorffs, Schinkels, Mendelsohns, Foersters and Matterns, but without imitating them. The aim, now as then, is to produce a horticultural and architectural work that attracts present interest and that will in future be counted among the best examples of both landscape architecture and architecture.

Civilian Potsdam may be the capital of the federal state of Brandenburg, but it is usually perceived as an excursion destination just outside Berlin. It is looking for a new identity and a new urban form while at the same time remaining the town of gardens, parks and palaces. As such large parts of Potsdam's urban landscape were declared a UNESCO World Heritage site in the 1990s. Of course this decision was disputed, both inside Potsdam and in the newspaper arts pages. A consistently critical attitude was maintained about individual building projects – from the new and truly banal Potsdam-Center by the station to the building of a tram-line through the Russian Alexandrowska housing estate to provide access to the new district of Bornstedter Feld – associated with threats of rescinding World Heritage status. Or at least this threat was anticipated in internal discussions. But then what isn't controversial in Potsdam, this favoured town that at the same time generates such sensitive and weighty emotions?

It was in precisely this situation that Potsdam set off to make its contribution to contemporary urban design and landscape architecture – to Garden Art between yesterday and tomorrow – and to present this contribution to the world at large on the occasion of the National Horticultural Show Potsdam 2001.

❶ In der Potsdamer Innenstadt zeigt sich die Freundschaftsinsel mit Staudenpflanzungen nach Plänen Karl Foersters sorgfältig restauriert.

Friendship Island in central Potsdam has been carefully restored with herbaceous planting on the basis of plans by Karl Foerster.

② Der 60 ha große Park im Bornstedter Feld ist das Herz einer insgesamt 300 ha großen städtebaulichen Entwicklungsmaßnahme im
Norden Potsdams. Stadtplätze markieren den Übergang zur Wohnbebauung.

The 60 hectare Park in the Bornstedter Feld is at the heart of an
urban development covering a total
of 300 ha in north Potsdam. Urban
squares mark the transition to residential areas.

③ Im Park wird ein Spiel mit Blicken
in die Potsdamer Kulturlandschaft
inszeniert. Im Gelände vorhandene
Wälle blieben erhalten, über sie
führen heute Wege mit vielfältigen
Blickbeziehungen.

A game with views of Potsdam's
parkland and gardens is staged in
the park. Embankments that were
in place on site are retained as
"ramparts", and today paths offering a wide range of linking views
run along them.

❶ Die militärische Vergangenheit des Bornstedter Feldes ist Gegenstand gestalterischer und künstlerischer Auseinandersetzung im neuen Park.

The Bornstedter Feld's military past becomes a focus for designers and artists in the new park.

❷ Camofields: Die Installation der Potsdamer Künstlergruppe BergWerk erinnert an die Potsdamer Militärgeschichte.

Camofields: this installation by BergWerk, a group of Potsdam artists, is a reminder of Potsdam's military past.

❸ Mit dem Auszug der sowjetischen Streitkräfte war die jahrhunderte-alte militärische Nutzung des Bornstedter Feldes beendet. Die Rote Kaserne ist ein Beispiel für die eindrucksvolle Militärarchitektur.

The departure of the Soviet forces marked the end of centuries of military use of the Bornstedter Feld. The Red Barracks is an example of impressive military architecture.

❶

❷

④

❶ Blickfang im Park sind die Staudentableaus, die bis zu 2 m aus dem
Boden ragen.

**The herbaceous tableaux, rising up
to two meters above the ground, are
an eye-catching feature in the park.**

❷ Während der Bauphase erinnerte
der Park aufgrund der Sicherung
militärgeschichtlicher Spuren an
eine Ausgrabungsstätte.

**The park looked like an archaeolog-
ical dig while traces of military history were being investigated during
the building phase.**

❸ Kunst im Park ist integraler Bestand-
teil des Entwurfskonzepts. Das topo-
graphisch gefaltete Basketballfeld
ist eine Arbeit der Berliner Künstlergruppe inges idee.

**Art in the park is an integral com-
ponent of the design concept. This
topographically challenged Basketball Court is the work of inges idee,
a group of artists based in Berlin.**

❹ Die Wälle schaffen eine eindrucksvolle Raumfolge im Park.

**The "ramparts" create an impressive
spatial sequence in the park.**

❶ Ein Obsthain schließt den Park im Bornstedter Feld nach Süden ab. Im Hintergrund der Pfingstberg östlich des Parks.

A grove of fruit trees forms the southern conclusion of the Park in the Bornstedter Feld. In the background, east of the park, is the Pfingstberg.

❷ „Baumhallen" bestimmen die Parkränder im Übergang zu den angrenzenden Stadtquartieren.

"Tree halls" mark the edges of the park at points of transition to adjacent urban quarters.

❸ Der neue Park bildet ein bisher fehlendes Verbindungsstück der historischen Gärten. Er leitet von Sanssouci und dem Ruinenberg über in die Lennésche Feldflur, zur russischen Siedlung Alexandrowka und zum Pfingstberg.

The new park provides a connection to the historic gardens that has previously been missing. It leads from Sanssouci and the Ruinenberg into the Bornstedt Meadowland, the Russian Alexandrowka housing estate and the Pfingstberg.

❹ Der Blick vom Ruinenberg nach Süden zeigt die historischen Anlagen am Schloß Sanssouci.

The view south from the Ruinenberg shows the historic gardens of Schloss Sanssouci.

❺ Im Norden der neue Park im Bornstedter Feld.

To the north is the new Park in the Bornstedter Feld.

❻ In der Feldflur nördlich Potsdams wurden wesentliche Elemente wie diese Allee rekonstruiert. Einst gestaltete Peter Joseph Lenné diese Feldflur, indem er landschaftskünstlerische und landwirtschaftliche Nutzungen verband.

Essential elements like this avenue were reconstructed in the Meadowland north of Potsdam. The Meadowland was formerly designed by Peter Joseph Lenné, who united the art of landscape and agricultural uses.

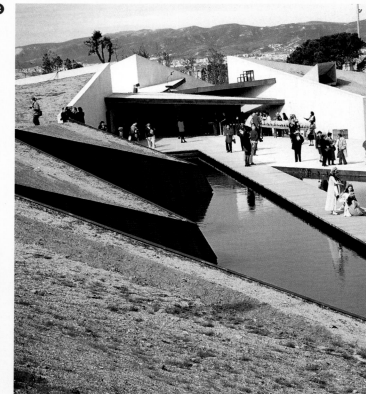

1 Der Landschaftspark Duisburg-Nord (Latz + Partner) – hier die „Piazza Metallica" zwischen den Hochöfen eines ehemaligen Stahlwerkes – wurde zum Inbegriff einer neuen Haltung der Landschaftsarchitektur: Vorhandene Relikte vorheriger Nutzungen werden integriert und gestalterisch betont.

The Duisburg-Nord landscape park (Latz + Partner) – this is the "Piazza Metallica" between the blast furnaces of a former steel works – became the epitome of a new approach to landscape architecture: remnants from the past and previous uses are incorporated and emphasized in the design.

2 Der neue Botanische Garten Barcelonas (Bet Figueras) inszeniert die vorhandene Topographie. Wände aus Corten-Stahl fangen die gefalteten Hänge ab.

Barcelona's new Botanical Garden (Bet Figueras) puts the existing topography on show. The folded slopes are shored up with Corten steel walls.

3 Für die Verbindung aus Design und Gartenkunst steht der Entwurf der jungen Landschaftsarchitekten GROSS. MAX (Edinburgh) für eine Landesgartenschau in Leverkusen.

The design by the young landscape architects GROSS. MAX (Edinburgh) for a Horticultural Show in Leverkusen shows how innovative design and garden art are linked.

4 Die Gartenschau Bad Oeynhausen / Löhne „Aqua Magica" wurde dank der Ideen der französischen Landschaftsarchitekten Agence Ter zum fröhlichen Festival des Wassers, das dem traditionellen Kurort neue Impulse gab.

The Bad Oeynhausen / Löhne Horticultural Show "Aqua Magica" became a joyous water festival that gave new impetus to the traditional spa, thanks to the French landscape architects Agence Ter.

4

Essay von **Gabriele Pütz**

Was ist ein zeitgemäßer Park (für Potsdam)?

Die Frage nach dem zeitgemäßen Park kann nicht eindeutig beantwortet werden. Ein Park läßt sich nicht anhand weniger Gestaltungsprinzipien oder Entwurfsmerkmale definieren. Zeitgenössische Parkanlagen sind in ihrer Gestalt, ihrer Materialität, ihrer Raumbildung und Funktionalität so vielschichtig und unterschiedlich wie nie. Hier spiegelt sich zum einen die Vielfalt der Anforderungen an einen Park, zum anderen die Vielfalt gestalterischer Möglichkeiten. Mit der Postmoderne wurde das Auseinanderfallen von Form und Funktion analysiert und propagiert. Doch es ist mehr noch die Uneindeutigkeit des Funktionsbegriffes in komplexen, medialen und postmechanistischen Gesellschaften, die jede Eindeutigkeit in der Beziehung zur Form unmöglich oder zumindest kaum noch als einfache, eindimensionale Ursache-Wirkung-Beziehung identifizierbar macht. Diese Komplexität des gesellschaftlichen Beziehungsgeflechtes kommt auch in den neu entstehenden Parkanlagen zum Ausdruck.

Bernard Tschumi, der mit dem Parc de la Villette in Paris den Prototyp des postmodernen Parks entwarf, hatte eigens Jacques Derrida, den Philosophen des Dekonstruktivismus, als Berater zugezogen und dennoch auf die „Verkündungsform" des Park-Kunstwerks als Ausdruck geistiger Haltungen zu gesellschaftlichen Verhältnissen zurückgegriffen. Latz + Partner dagegen versuchen, Komplexität nicht nur abzubilden, sondern zu gestalten. Wenn in ihren Entwürfen Systeme entwickelt und dargestellt werden, arbeiten sie physische Kreisläufe ebenso wie geschichtliche Entwicklungen ein.

Anstelle einer umfassenden Definition sollen hier zwei Aspekte herausgegriffen werden, die bei der Debatte um den zeitgemäßen Park relevant sind: zum einen der Gemeinsinn, das Erleben eines Zugehörigkeitsgefühls, ohne die Individualität aufgeben zu müssen, und zum anderen die Erfahrung von Komplexität und Dynamik.

Gemeinsinn

Einen neuen Park in Potsdam zu bauen, war eine besondere Herausforderung. Denn der neue Park muß sich jetzt und zukünftig an den historischen Parkanlagen messen lassen.

Wozu brauchen wir neue Parkanlagen? Was gibt uns ein Park, was wir nicht auch im Fitneßstudio, vor dem Fernseher oder auf Mallorca finden können? Der Medienwissenschaftler Norbert Bolz spricht von „Sinnesangeboten". Die Sinnfrage entstehe als Reaktion auf die „Krise der Identität" und die „hohe Komplexität der Gesellschaft", die ihren Ausdruck finde in der Diskrepanz von Form und Funktion. Reaktion auf die Sinnfrage sind „Sinnangebote" wie Spiritualität, Sport, Medien, Ökologie, Konsum, mittels derer die „Unüberschaubarkeit der Welt" „versüßt" werden soll. Ein Park kann solche Sinnangebote gebündelt anbieten, aber im besten Fall mehr sein als eine „Versüßung" – nämlich Ort des Sinnierens wie des sinnlichen Erlebens selbst.

Peter Latz bezeichnet den von ihm konzipierten „Park im Bornstedter Feld" als „neuen Volkspark". Eine Charakterisierung, die zunächst irritiert, da sie an die Volksparkbewegung zu Anfang des 20. Jahrhunderts erinnert. Die Spannung liegt jedoch gerade in der Neuinterpretation als Volkspark des 21. Jahrhunderts.

Volkspark verweist zunächst darauf, daß dieser Park nicht für Eliten gemacht ist, sondern daß es sich um einen öffentlichen Park handelt. Öffentlich zugänglich aber sind auch historische Parks – seit langem. Allerdings ist der Referenzpunkt ein anderer. Der heutige Park ist nicht mehr Ausdruck des Bewußtseins eines Herrschers, sondern Ausdruck einer demokratisch legitimierten Erwartungshaltung an Freiräume. Diese Erwartungen sind heterogen und deshalb durch eine paternalistische Haltung des guten Staates, des guten Bürgermeisters, Planungsbeamten oder Fabrikbesitzers, der seinem Volk einen Park spendiert, nicht mehr zu erfüllen. So stellt sich also bei einer Neuinterpretation des Volksparks zu Beginn des 21. Jahrhunderts die Frage: Wer ist das Volk?

Seit 1989 wissen wir wieder: Wir sind das Volk. Nur wer sind wir? Wer gehört dazu und wer nicht? Der Volksbegriff ist fragwürdig geworden, wie sich nicht zuletzt in der Debatte um das Kunstwerk „Der Bevölkerung" des Künstlers Hans Haake für das Reichstagsgebäude, dem Sitz des Deutschen Bundestages in Berlin, zeigt. Das „wir" zerfällt heute in viele kleine und große Interessengruppen, die sich aufgrund eines gemeinsamen Interesses zum temporären oder partiellen „wir" zusammenfinden, dieses Interesse verfolgen und dann auseinandergehen bzw. neue, andere Interessengruppen bilden. Der Übergang von der Volksgemeinschaft, Klassen- oder Kollektivgesellschaft zur Koexistenzgesellschaft führt zu Verunsicherungen. Jeder möchte dazu gehören, ohne genau zu wissen, wozu eigentlich.

Der zeitgemäße Volkspark ist kein politisches Rezept gegen die Sinnkrise. Dennoch kann ein attraktiv gestalteter Park subtil wirkende Botschaft und Potentialraum für eine Gemeinschaft der Individuen sein. Der Park bietet die Möglichkeit, das selten gewordene Gefühl von Gemeinschaft und Verbundenheit – und zwar zu Mensch und Natur – zu erfahren. Das Besondere besteht darin, daß diese Erfahrung im Park ungezwungen möglich ist, da Individualität und persönliche Freiheit nicht aufgegeben werden müssen. Im Gegenteil: Individuelle Freiheit im Spiel der Einbildungskraft ist Voraussetzung zum Erleben von Schönheit und dem damit intendierten Verbundenheitsgefühl.

Ich sitze auf der Parkbank, betrachte die Schönheit der Blüten, freue mich über den Wiesenraum und die den Raum abrundende Baumkulisse. Ich genieße das Wohlgefühl angesichts der Schönheit dieser Situation. Mit der Frau, die langsam an mir vorbeispaziert, wechsle ich einen flüchtigen Blick. In ihren Augen erkenne ich eine Freude wieder, die auch ich angesichts der Schönheit der Situation empfinde. In diesem Moment fühle ich mich dieser Person verbunden. Es entsteht ein Wir-Gefühl allein dadurch, daß wir feststellen, daß beide dieselbe Situation als schön empfinden.

Etwas schön zu finden, ein Geschmacksurteil zu fällen, ist eine kulturelle Leistung. Der Park fordert zu dieser Leistung heraus. Die Feststellung, daß auch andere dieses Schönheitsempfinden teilen, vermittelt die Gewißheit einer kulturellen Zugehörigkeit bzw. Verbundenheit. Der Park, den ich mir individuell aneignen kann und der gleichzeitig offen ist, nicht vereinnahmt von Nutzen, Funktionen und gesellschaftlichen Zwängen, ermöglicht es auf spielerisch leichte Art, eher zufällig, ein Gemeinschaftsgefühl aufzubauen, ohne die Individualität aufgeben zu müssen. Interesseloses Wohlgefallen heißt diese Voraussetzung des Empfindens von Schönheit, des ästhetischen Urteils, bei Kant.

Komplexität und Dynamik

Die weltweiten Zusammenhänge und die gesellschaftlichen Verhältnisse sind so komplex, daß wir sie nicht als Ganzes erklären können. Auch weil uns die Worte und Bilder fehlen. Nochmals Bolz: „Die sogenannte

Sinnkrise ist also zunächst einmal nur ein Hinweis darauf, daß wir unsere Gegenwart mit den alten Begriffen nicht mehr zureichend beschreiben können. Die uns vertraute Semantik ... taugt nicht mehr zur Weltbeschreibung." Taugt also „Volkspark" noch? Ja und nein! Die Komplexität von Gesellschaft und Welt läßt es heute nicht mehr opportun erscheinen, nur eine Idee, ein Ideal, ein Leitbild in einem Park zu verwirklichen. Bei der Gestaltung, Nutzung und Interpretation eines Parks ist es daher nicht angebracht, nur in eine Richtung zu denken, wenn der Park den Anspruch erfüllen soll, im Sinne eines zeitgemäßen „Volksparks" den Wünschen und Anforderungen möglichst aller Parkbesucher gerecht zu werden.

Der Park selbst ist ein komplexes System. In ihm spielen vielfältige Faktoren wie Pflanzen, Boden, Wasser, Luft, Farbe und Duft, Jahreszeiten, optische und haptische Erlebnisse und nicht zuletzt die Parkbesucher zu einem komplexen System der Geschmacksbildung zusammen. Der Park ist durchdrungen von natürlichen Prozessen und menschlichen Interventionen. Gleichzeitig ist der Park kein Ding. Er ist nicht statisch, sondern unterliegt einer eigenen Dynamik von Wachsen und Vergehen, die zum Beispiel im Wechsel der Jahreszeiten konkret erfahrbar wird. Dynamische Prozesse sind im Park als stabiler Augenblick wie als Veränderung in unterschiedlichen Geschwindigkeiten erlebbar.

Damit kann ein Park heutigen Empfindungen von Komplexität und Dynamik Ausdruck geben, ohne das Gefühl permanenter Überforderung auszulösen. Park beruhigt, nicht als Seditativum, sondern als Ausdruck der Teilhabe an selbstreferentiellen Prozessen. Das Parkerlebnis relativiert Alltags- und Sonntagserfahrungen, als Freiraum wie als Bezugsraum.

Flexibilität und Dynamik eines zeitgemäßen Volksparks sind wichtig – und in seiner Gestaltung zu berücksichtigen –, um die vielfältigen und unterschiedlichen Interessen der Parkbesucher ungezwungen nebeneinander zu ermöglichen. Die Bedeutung von Flexibilität und Dynamik im Park geht jedoch darüber hinaus. Ein wesentliches Merkmal und eine besondere Qualität des Parks besteht darin, daß Komplexität, Dynamik und Prozeßhaftigkeit – wesentliche Parameter unserer heutigen Gesellschaft – im Park zu erfahren sind. Durch das konkrete Erleben von gesellschaftlichen Prinzipien (von Zeitgeist) kann ich zwar nicht verstehen, jedoch erfahren, was Gesellschaft, was Gemeinschaft heute bedeutet. Die romantische Alternative dagegen, die „Suche nach dem verlorenen Sinn", ist eigentlich nur „eine Flucht aus der Komplexität" (Bolz). Der Park allein als Fluchtort (was er auch ist) wäre zu wenig. In der Bedeutung als Reflexionsraum liegt die zweite wesentliche Ebene des zeitgemäßen Parks.

Gabriele Pütz ist mit dem Landschaftsarchitekturbüro Gruppe F, Berlin, für die Rahmenplanung des Parks im Bornstedter Feld verantwortlich.

Essay by **Gabriele Pütz**

What sort of park do we need (for Potsdam) today?

It is not possible to give a definite answer to the question about a park that would be in keeping today. A park cannot be defined by naming a few creative principles or key design features. Contemporary parks are as complex and diverse in their form, material qualities, spatial effects and general functions as they have ever been. This reflects both the wide range of demands made on a park and also the wide range of creative possibilities. Post-Modernism meant that a new disparity of form and function was analysed and promoted. But it is much more the ambiguity of the concept of function in complex media and post-mechanical societies that makes any unambiguity in relation to form impossible or at least no longer identifiable as a simple, one-dimensional cause and effect relationship. This complex web of social relations is also expressed in the new parks.

Bernard Tschumi, who designed the prototype of the post-Modern park in the Parc de la Villette in Paris, specially consulted Jacques Derrida, the philosopher of Deconstructivism, to this end, and nevertheless went back to the "proclamation" form of the park as a work of art, an expression of intellectual attitudes to social conditions. By contrast, Latz + Partner are not just trying to illustrate complexity, they are trying to create it. When systems are developed and presented in their designs, they work in both physical cycles and historical developments.

Rather than attempting a comprehensive definition, we intend to isolate two aspects here that are relevant to the debate about contemporary parks: one is community spirit, the experience of a sense of belonging without having to abandon one's individuality, and the other is the experience of complexity and dynamics.

Community spirit

Creating a new park in Potsdam was a particular challenge, as this new park will have to be measured against historical parks, now and in the future.

Why do we need new parks? What do we get from a park that we could not find in the gym, on television or on Mallorca? Media theorist Norbert Bolz speaks of "supplies of meaning". He says that the search for meaning arises as a reaction to the "crisis of identity" and our "highly complex society", as expressed in the discrepancy between form and function. "Supplies of meaning" like spirituality, sport, media, ecology, consumerism, intended to "sweeten" the "unmanageability of the world", are responses to this question. A park can offer such supplies of meaning in concentrated form, but in the best case be more than a "sweetener" – in fact a place for musing as well as sensual experience.

Peter Latz describes his Park in the Bornstedter Feld as a "new people's park". This is a somewhat unsettling description at first, as it summons up the people's park movement in the early 20th century. But the excitement lies precisely in re-interpreting the idea as a 21st century people's park.

The people's park concept alludes first to the fact that this park is not intended for élites, but that it is a public park. Historical parks, too, have been open to the public – for a long time. Yet the reference point is a different one. Modern parks do not express a ruler's consciousness, but express a democratically legitimate attitude: we expect there to be open spaces. These expectations are heterogeneous and thus can no longer be fulfilled by a paternalistic attitude taken by a good state, a good mayor, planning official or factory owner who gives his people a park. And so as the people's park is re-interpreted at the beginning of the 21st century the question arises: who are the people?

We have known the answer to this again since 1989: we are the people. But who are we? Who belongs and who doesn't? The concept of the people has become questionable, as was not least shown in the debate about the work of art called "Der Bevölkerung" (To the Population) by the artist Hans Haake for the Reichstag, the seat of the German parliament in Berlin. Today "we" breaks down into large and small groups of interested parties, who come together to form a temporary or a partial "we" on the basis of a common interest. They pursue this interest, then split up again or form new and different special interest groups. The transition from the national community, class or collective society to the co-existence society leads to a sense of insecurity. Everyone wants to belong, without knowing precisely what (they want to belong) to.

The contemporary people's park is not a political remedy for the crisis in meaning. But an attractively designed park can be a subtly effective message and potential space for a community of individuals. Parks offer the possibility of experiencing what is now a rare feeling of community and closeness – between both people and nature. The special feature is that this experience can be had quite naturally in a park, as individuality and personal freedom do not have to be abandoned. On the contrary: individual liberty in giving our imagination free play is essential if we are to experience beauty and the feeling of closeness and attachment that this implies.

I sit on the park bench, admire the beauty of the flowers, enjoy the area of grass and the background of trees that rounds off the space. I revel in the feeling of well-being that I derive from the beauty of this situation. I exchange a fleeting glance with the woman who walks slowly past me. I recognize a delight in her eyes that I also feel here. I feel close to this person at this moment. We both have a sense of "we" simply because we establish that we both find the same situation beautiful.

Finding something beautiful, making a judgement in terms of taste, is a cultural action. The park challenges us to perform this action. Finding out that other people share this sense of beauty as well conveys the certainty of belonging and being close culturally. The park, which I can acquire as an individual and that is at the same time open, not monopolized by uses, functions and social constraints, makes it easily possible to build up a feeling of community almost by chance, without having to abandon individuality. In terms of the philospher Kant, a state of disinterested well-being is the pre-requisite for sensing beauty, for aesthetic judgement.

Complexity and dynamics
World-wide connections and social relationships are so complex that we cannot explain them as a whole. This is also because we are short of words and images. Bolz again: "And so the so-called crisis in meaning is first of all just an indication that we can no longer adequately describe our present by using the old concepts. The familiar semantics . . . are no longer any good for describing the world." So is "people's park" still any good? Yes and no! The complexity of society and the world means that it no longer seems

opportune to realize just one idea, one ideal, one model in a park. Thus when designing, using and interpreting a park, it is not appropriate to think along one track only if the park is to meet the wishes and demands of as many visitors as possible.

The park itself is a complex system. In it a large number of factors – plants, soil, water, air, colour and fragrance, the seasons, visual and tactile experiences, and not least the visitors to the park themselves – come together to form a complex system for shaping taste. The park is permeated with natural processes and human interventions. At the same time the park is not a thing. It is not static, but subject to its own dynamic of growth and decay, which can be experienced in a concrete fashion in the changing seasons, for example. Dynamic processes can be experienced in the park as a stable moment and as a change taking place at different speeds.

Thus a park can express current senses of complexity and dynamics, without triggering a feeling of being permanently overtaxed. A park is calming, not as a sedative but as an expression of participating in a self-referential process. The park experience relativizes everyday and Sunday experiences, as an open space and as a referential space.

The flexibility and dynamics of an up-to-date people's park are important – and should be taken into consideration at the design stage – in order to make it possible for the diverse and different interests of the park visitors to evolve naturally alongside each other. But the meaning of flexibility and dynamics in the park goes beyond this. A key feature and a special quality of a park is that complexity, dynamics and processuality – essential parameters in our current society – can be experienced there. I cannot understand, but I can experience, through concrete contact with social principles, with Zeitgeist, what society, what community means today. The romantic alternative to this, the "search for the lost meaning" is actually only "a flight from complexity" (Bolz). The park as a mere place of refuge (which it also is) would be too little. The second essential plane of the contemporary park lies in its significance as a place for reflection.

Gabriele Pütz is responsible, with the Gruppe F landscape architecture practice, for the overall planning of the Park in the Bornstedter Feld.

Die Insel Potsdam – Ideal einer Kulturlandschaft

Mit launigen Schiffsfahrten des Großen Kurfürsten begann im 17. Jahrhundert der Aufstieg des kleinen Fleckens an der Furt durch die Havel zur preußischen Residenzstadt Potsdam. Wasser und die Sehnsucht nach einer Atmosphäre, die von idealen Bildern beherrscht wird, bestimmen seither die Gestalt der Stadt, die nicht ohne Verklärung „Insel Potsdam" genannt wird.

Der Große Kurfürst ließ im nördlich des Flusses liegenden Sumpfgebiet Brücken und Dämme errichten und schuf so den Grund für die planmäßige Errichtung Potsdams. Unter seinen Nachfolgern wurde die erste und zweite barocke Stadterweiterung in Angriff genommen, zu denen die drei frühen Beispiele sogenannten „Stadtgrüns", nämlich Wilhelmplatz (heute Platz der Einheit), Plantage und Bassinplatz gehören. Friedrich der Große festigte im 18. Jahrhundert mit Sanssouci und seinem abseits der Politik geführten Lebensstil die Imagination von Potsdam als Ort der Kontemplation. Ein Leitbild, das unter Friedrich Wilhelm IV. in der ersten Hälfte des 19. Jahrhunderts zu einer umfassenden, an italienischen Landschaftseindrücken orientierten „Welt en miniature" baulich umgesetzt wurde. Dieser preußische König begründete mit der Förderung und Unterstützung seiner königlichen Hofgärtner und Baumeister Peter Joseph Lenné, Karl Friedrich Schinkel und Ludwig Persius das wohl umfassendste gestalterische Vorhaben für Potsdam, nämlich die Realisierung einer gartenkünstlerisch-architektonischen „Kulturlandschaft" im Sinne eines Gesamtkunstwerks.

Die Stadt wandelte sich freilich nicht zu einem fantastischen Satelliten. Parallel zur „Landesverschönerung" wurde Potsdam bis ins 20. Jahrhundert als Hauptstandort des deutschen Militärs ausgebaut. Die Könige, später die Kaiser und zuletzt die Nationalsozialisten errichteten große Kasernen vor allem im Norden der Stadt. Die am 21. März 1933 in der Garnisonkirche inszenierte „Versöhnung" der Nationalsozialisten mit dem preußischen Militär fand nicht von ungefähr als „Tag von Potsdam" Eingang in die Geschichte. Nach dem Zweiten Weltkrieg belegten die sowjetischen Alliierten die Standorte, teilweise bis Mitte der neunziger Jahre. Heute residiert die Bundeswehr, unter anderem mit dem Militärgeschichtlichen Forschungsamt, in einigen traditionellen Gebäuden der Streitmächte in Potsdam.

Den Gartenkünstlern jedoch gelang es, ihre Anlagen abseits von militärischen Erfordernissen zu errichten, so daß die soldatische Seite der Stadt den romantischen Begriff der „Insel Potsdam" nicht schmälerte. 200 Jahre lang formten sie aus Seen, Sümpfen, Wäldern und auf kargen Böden den heute einzigartigen Landschaftsraum, der unzweifelhaft eine einmalige Kulturleistung ist. „Einige, die sich über Zusammenhänge in der menschlichen Landschaft – vor allem über die Folgen des Bewahrens der Erde dieser Gesellschaft – Gedanken machen" – mit diesem Satz von Hermann Mattern lassen sich die Handelnden unterschiedlicher Epochen auf einen Nenner bringen.

Der Ursprung des Konzepts einer großen, Stadt und Landschaft integrierenden „Kulturlandschaft" lag bei dem Direktor der königlichen Gärten, Peter Joseph Lenné. Sein „Verschönerungsplan" von 1833 gilt bis heute als ideelles, wenngleich überholtes Ziel der Potsdamer Gartenkunst. Unter Berücksichtigung landwirtschaftlicher und finanzieller Aspekte setzte Lenné die umgebende Landschaft in Beziehung zu Stadt und Parks. Zur Vollkommenheit gebracht wurde die Landschaftsgestaltung durch Bauten der Architekten Karl Friedrich Schinkel und Ludwig Persius: Monumente wie die Potsdamer Nikolaikirche, die Bornstedter Kirche, der Normannische Turm auf dem Ruinenberg oder das Gut Bornstedt sind durch ein Geflecht von Blickbeziehungen weithin in der Landschaft sichtbar.

Lenné überformte auch die regelmäßigen Anlagen des Parkes Sanssouci im Stil des englischen Landschaftsgartens. Denn das barocke Prinzip der Beugung des natürlichen Wuchses in eine ornamentale Ordnung widersprach sowohl dem rationalen Gedankengut der Aufklärung als auch der einsetzenden romantischen Hinwendung zur Natur. Auch die gestalterische Öffnung des königlichen Parks zur Landschaft erscheint im Angesicht der Revolution von 1848 wie die gestalterische Entsprechung zum gesellschaftlichen Wandel von der Feudal- zur Bürgergesellschaft – einem Wandel, der sich letztlich in den „Volkspark"-Entwürfen des 20. Jahrhunderts manifestierte.

Getragen von dem rationalen Wissen um den Landschaftsbau entsprach das Vorgehen Lennés dem eines Ingenieurs, der um die Bedeutung von Lehre und Grundlagenvermittlung wußte. In diesem Bewußtsein begründete Lenné die Königliche Gärtnerlehranstalt zu Schöneberg und Potsdam, an der die erste wissenschaftliche Ausbildung zum Gärtner in Europa angeboten wurde. Doch Lennés idealistische Gartenlehre war von Beginn an umstritten, besonders unter preußischen Gutsbesitzern, die „einen Garten als ein nothwendiges Uebel betrachten, das Kost macht und wenig oder nichts rendirt". Die Weichenstellungen zwischen „Kunst" und „Wirtschaft" blieben immer ein Streitpunkt, der die Schule bis zur Übersiedlung in den späteren Berliner Bezirk Dahlem im Jahr 1903 verfolgte.

Der Geist Lennés beherrschte das Jahrhundert seines Wirkens. Erst im 20. Jahrhundert begann eine neue und eigenständige Periode Potsdamer Gartenkunst: mit dem Bornimer Kreis. Sein Ausgangs- und Mittelpunkt war Karl Foerster, ein Staudenzüchter, Philosoph, Metaphysiker und Gärtner. Foerster empfand als Pantheist höchsten Respekt vor jedem Lebewesen: „Die Liebe zur Pflanze und zur Besonderheit der Pflanze", lautete seine Botschaft. Mit ihr verstand er es, Menschen für seine Hingabe zur Natur zu begeistern. Das Haus Foersters ist seit jeher ein sozialer Treffpunkt gewesen, es stand – wie Schüler und Praktikanten berichten – für alle offen. In der um 1930 gegründeten Arbeitsgemeinschaft mit den Landschaftsarchitekten Herta Hammerbacher und Hermann Mattern wurden mehrere Projekte in Potsdam entwickelt, denen Foersters Ideen von der Harmonie der Pflanzenwelt zugrunde lagen. Seine Gärtnerei mit dem berühmten Senkgarten in Bornim sowie der Schau- und Sichtungsgarten auf der Freundschaftsinsel tragen diesen Geist bis in die Gegenwart.

Dem Bornimer Kreis gehörten ehemalige Schüler Foersters an, die sich aus dem Umfeld der Arbeitsgemeinschaft rekrutierten. Nach dem Zweiten Weltkrieg wurden die Ansätze bei regelmäßigen Treffen in Bornim fortentwickelt. Vor allem die Landschaftsarchitekten und Foerster-Schüler Walter Funcke und Hermann Göritz unterstützten die Ideen und die Pflanzenzüchtungen Foersters in der Phase nach der Gründung des zweiten deutschen Staates. Die DDR nahm das Erbe des als Pazifisten ausgewiesenen Staudengärtners an, wodurch die Werke Foersters gefördert und gepflegt wurden. Wie die weltberühmten Potsdamer Schlösser und Gärten wurden sie als Traditionsinseln bewahrt, denen man aufgrund ihres Alters und ihrer natürlichen Pracht Respekt zollte.

Anders verhielten sich die Regierenden der DDR bis in die achtziger Jahre gegenüber allem, was mit dem Staat Preußen zu tun hatte. Der „Tag von Potsdam" wurde den staatstragenden Bauten der Kaiserzeit zum Verhängnis. Namentlich die Ruine des Potsdamer Stadtschlosses und der erhalten gebliebene Turm der Garnisonkirche wurden spät, nämlich in den sechziger Jahren, als Symbole des preußischen Militarismus gesprengt.

Dabei hatte die öffentliche Verwaltung schon 1951, kurz nach Gründung des zweiten deutschen Staates, mit ersten Rekonstruktionsmaßnahmen an den Bürgerhäusern entlang der Friedrich-Ebert-Straße begonnen; die Sanierung setzte sich bis 1989 sukzessive fort – wenn auch nicht flächendeckend. In anderen Gebieten trug Potsdam dem zeitgenössischen Gedanken des aufgelockerten Städtebaus genauso Rechnung wie jede vergleichbare Stadt im internationalen Rahmen. Die heute befremdende Brutalität, mit der die Schneise „Lange Brücke – Friedrich-Ebert-Straße" in die Innenstadt geschlagen wurde, beruhte auf einer in den sechziger Jahren üblichen Wertschätzung der verkehrlichen Belange.

Die Planung der südlich des Stadtkanals und westlich des Lustgartens liegenden Bereiche erfolgte ohne grundlegende Konzeption. Nach Schleifung des Stadtschlosses, dem Wiederaufbau der Nikolaikirche sowie des Alten Rathauses und des Knobelsdorffhauses als städtisches Kulturhaus und schließlich dem Neubau des Instituts für Lehrerbildung (heute Fachhochschule) sollte ein gesellschaftliches Zentrum im Bereich des Alten Marktes entstehen. Der Weimarer Bauhistoriker Thomas Topfstedt resümierte 1988: „Jedenfalls gelang es nicht, die durch Kriegseinwirkung und nachfolgende Flächenberäumungen entstandenen Raumschneisen mit städtebaulichen Neuschöpfungen von Rang zu schließen." Erst Ende der achtziger Jahre wurde die offene Flanke zur Havel in Form eines Theaterbaus geschlossen; dieser befand sich zur Zeit des Mauerfalls 1989 jedoch erst im Rohbau und wurde zu Beginn der neunziger Jahre abgetragen.

Nach dem Wegfall dogmatischer Planungsvorgaben geraten in Potsdam unweigerlich die unterschiedlichen Prioritäten in Konflikt. Eine wirtschaftlich erfolgreiche Stadt wollen die einen, das landschaftliche Ideal wiederherstellen die anderen, eine weitere Gruppe sucht nach einer neuen Identität, und zurückgekehrte Potsdamer bemängeln den Kleingeist ihrer nunmehr zur Landeshauptstadt Brandenburgs ernannten Heimat.

Die erste Bewertung der Landschaft Potsdams und von Teilen seines Stadtgebiets als Weltkulturerbe durch die UNESCO im Jahr 1990 erscheint vielen als Signal gegen jegliche Neubauten, die freilich – wie das Potsdam-Center am Hauptbahnhof – nicht mehr rückgängig zu machen sind. Das trifft zumindest mittelfristig auch auf viele andere Gebiete der Stadt zu und wird neue, immer spezifischere Debatten erfordern. Rekonstruktion hin, das Recht auf zeitgenössische Gestaltung her – „Erbe der Kultur" könnte hier heißen, die Besonderheit Potsdams als imaginierter Ort – Italien zu Zeiten der Könige, Harmonie und der Respekt vor der Natur im 20. Jahrhundert – im 21. Jahrhundert erneut zu beleben.

Potsdam Island – the ideal park landscape

Originally a little hamlet by a ford over the Havel river, Potsdam started to rise to the status of Royal Prussian Residence in the 17th century, when the Great Elector amused himself by taking boat trips there. Water and a desire for an atmosphere dominated by ideal images have defined the shape of the town ever since, which is known, not without a sense of transfiguration, as "Insel Potsdam" – Potsdam Island.

The Great Elector had bridges and causeways built in the marshy area north of the river, thus creating the land on which Potsdam was to be planned and built. The first and second Baroque expansions took place under his successors, including the three early examples of "green public space", which were Wilhelmplatz (now Platz der Einheit), Plantage and Bassinplatz. Frederick the Great established the idea of Potsdam as a place of contemplation in the 18th century with Sanssouci, and his life conducted away from the political scene. This was a model that was implemented by architectural means under Friedrich Wilhelm IV in the first half of the 19th century in the form of a comprehensive "world en miniature", following impressions of the Italian landscape. This Prussian king, encouraged and supported by his royal court gardeners and architects Peter Joseph Lenné, Karl Friedrich Schinkel and Ludwig Persius, set up what was probably the most extensive design project for Potsdam – to use the art of gardens and of buildings for realizing a park landscape in the form of a Gesamtkunstwerk, a universal work of art.

Yet the town was not transformed into a dreamy satellite. In parallel with this "beautification of the land", Potsdam expanded as the main home of the German armed forces well into the 20th century. The kings, later the emperors and finally the National Socialists built large barracks, above all in the northern part of the town. It was no coincidence that the National Socialists' "reconciliation" with the Prussian military, staged on 21 March 1933 in the Garnisonkirche, went down in history as "Day of Potsdam". After the Second World War the Soviet allies took over these locations, occupying some of them until the mid-nineties. Today the German armed forces are using some of the traditional military buildings for a number of purposes, including the Military history research office.

But the landscape architects managed to establish their sites well away from any military requirements, so that the soldierly side of the town did not detract from the romantic concept of "Potsdam Island". For 200 years they created the present unique landscape from lakes, marshes and woods and on poor soil. There is no doubt that this was an unparalleled cultural achievement. A statement by landscape architect Hermann Mattern defined a common denominator for all those involved at different periods – "people who ponder over connections in the human landscape – above all over the consequences of preserving the earth of this society".

The origin of the concept of a large park landscape, integrating town and countryside, lay with the director of the royal gardens, Peter Joseph Lenné. His 1833 "Beautification Plan" is still seen as an icon of Potsdam Garden Art, though it is no longer up-to-date. Lenné related the surrounding landscape to the town and parks, taking agricultural and financial aspects into consideration. The landscape design was brought to perfection by the buildings of architects Karl Friedrich Schinkel and Ludwig Persius: monuments like the Nikolaikirche in Potsdam, the Bornstedt church, the Norman Tower on the Ruinenberg or the Bornstedt estate are visible over long distances through a whole network of related views.

Lenné also reshaped the regular layout of the Sanssouci park in the style of English landscape gardens. The Baroque principle of bending natural growth into ornamental order contradicted both the rational thinking of the Enlightenment and also the incipient Romantic inclination towards nature. And the design device of opening up the royal park to the countryside, seen in the context of the 1848 revolution, seems like a creative reflection of the social change from a feudal to a bourgeois society – a change that was ultimately to lead to the "people's park" designs of the 20th century. Supported by rational knowledge about agriculture, Lenné's approach was like that of an engineer who knows about the significance of theory and conveying basic essentials. It was in this spirit that Lenné founded the Königliche Gärtnerlehranstalt zu Schöneberg und Potsdam (Schöneberg and Potsdam royal gardening educational institute), which offered the first academic horticultural training course in Europe. But Lenné's idealist horticultural theories were controversial from the outset, especially among Prussian landowners, who "see a garden as a necessary evil that causes expense and yields little or nothing". The choice of direction between "art" and "commerce" remained a controversial point which the school pursued until it moved to what was later to become the Berlin district of Dahlem in 1903.

The spirit of Lenné dominated the century in which he worked. It was not until the 20th century that a new and independent period started for Potsdam garden history: with the Bornimer Kreis (Bornim circle). Its initiator and focal point was Karl Foerster, a grower of herbaceous perennials, philosopher, metaphysician and gardener. As a pantheist, Foerster felt the highest possible respect for all living creatures: his message was "love of plants and the particular qualities of plants", and he knew to make people enthusiastic about nature. Foerster's house was always a social meeting-place that – as pupils and trainees report – was open to all. Several projects based on Foerster's ideas of the harmony of the plant world were developed in Potsdam by the team founded in 1930 with landscape architects Herta Hammerbacher and Hermann Mattern. Foerster's nursery and famous sunken garden in Bornim and the specimen garden on the Freundschaftsinsel carry this spirit into the present.

The Bornim circle included some of Foerster's pupils, recruited from associates of the team. After the Second World War the early work was developed further at regular meetings in Bornim. It was above all the landscape architects and pupils of Foerster, Walter Funcke and Hermann Göritz who supported Foerster's ideas and plant breeds in the phase after the foundation of the second German state. The GDR took over the legacy of this particular gardener, who had a reputation as a pacifist, which meant that Foerster's work was promoted and fostered. Like the world-famous Potsdam palaces and gardens, his creations were preserved as islands of tradition that deserved respect because of their age and natural splendour.

The rulers of the GDR behaved differently right into the eighties as far as anything that had to do with the state of Prussia was concerned. The above-mentioned "Day of Potsdam" was the doom of the state buildings of the imperial age. The ruined Potsdam Stadtschloss and the surviving tower of the Garnisonkirche in particular were blown up at a very late stage, in fact in the sixties, as symbols of Prussian militarism.

But in contrast with this, the authorities started their first rebuilding measures to the town houses in Friedrich-Ebert-Strasse as early as 1951, shortly after the second German state was founded; they were successively refurbished up to 1989 – though not comprehensively. In other areas Potsdam paid just as much attention to the contemporary idea of varied urban development as any comparable town in the international context. The brutal way, which we find astonishing now, in which the line of Lange Brücke and Friedrich-Ebert-Strasse was smashed through the city centre derived from the predominant sixties sense that traffic needs were more important than historical ones.

Planning the areas south of the Stadtkanal and west of the Lustgarten was carried out with no underlying concept. After the Stadtschloss had been razed to the ground, the Nikolaikirche rebuilt, along with the Old Town Hall and the Knobelsdorff House as a municipal house of culture, and finally a new building for the Teacher Training Institute (now a specialist college), a social centre was to have been established in the area of the Alter Markt. The Weimar architectural historian Thomas Topfstedt summed up in 1988: "In any case it proved impossible to close up the empty spaces caused by the war and subsequent large-scale clearance with high-quality new urban development." It was not until the late eighties that the open flank on the Havel side was closed with a theatre; this was a mere shell when the Wall fell in 1989, and was demolished in the early nineties.

Once dogmatic planning guidelines had disappeared the various priorities in Potsdam inevitably came into conflict. Some wanted a commercially successful town, others wanted to restore the landscape ideals, and yet another group was looking for a new identity, and Potsdam people who had returned to the town were disappointed by the small-mindedness of their home, which was now the capital of Brandenburg.

When UNESCO first named Potsdam's landscape and part of the city a World Heritage Site in 1990, this was seen by many people as a warning sign of resistance to some new buildings that in fact – like the Potsdam-Center near the main station – are definitely here to stay. This concerns, at least in the medium term, many other areas of the town as well, and will require new and ever more specific debates. Reconstruction or the right to contemporary design – in this case World Heritage could mean a 21st century revival of Potsdam's special qualities as a place created by imagination – with reference to Italy at the time of the kings, and to harmony and respect for nature in the 20th century.

1 Das einstige, weltberühmte Panorama Potsdams wurde vom Stadtschloß und der Nikolaikirche bestimmt; hier um 1905 vom Brauhausberg aus gesehen.

Potsdam's former, world-famous panorama was dominated by the Stadtschloss and the Nikolaikirche, seen here from the Brauhausberg in about 1905.

2 Der Blick vom Brauhausberg auf die expandierende Stadt zeigt bereits in der ersten Hälfte des 18. Jahrhunderts ihre Wahrzeichen Garnisonkirche, Stadtschloß und Nikolaikirche, Heilig-Geist-Kirche (von links nach rechts); Kupferstich 1735 – 1737.

The view from the Brauhausberg across the expanding town showed its familiar landmarks already in the first half of the 18th century: Garnisonkirche, Stadtschloss and Nikolaikirche, Heilig-Geist-Kirche (from left to right); copperplate engraving 1735 – 1737.

3 Der historische Stadtplan von Potsdam im Jahr 1683 zeigt die Entwicklung der räumlichen Situation am Alten Markt; die kleinteilige Struktur wird von den Stadterweiterungen, hier bis 1797 dargestellt, überlagert.

Potsdam's historic town plan in 1683 shows the space around the Old Market developing; the intricate structure is overlaid with the town expansion, shown here to 1797.

4 Der aktuelle Blick vom Hotel Mercure erfaßt die städtebauliche Situation am Standort des ehemaligen Stadtschlosses. In den nächsten Jahren soll die Situation wieder an den historischen Stadtgrundriss angenähert werden.

The current view from the Hotel Mercure shows urban development on the site of the former Stadtschloss. The historic ground plan will be reverted to within the next few years.

1

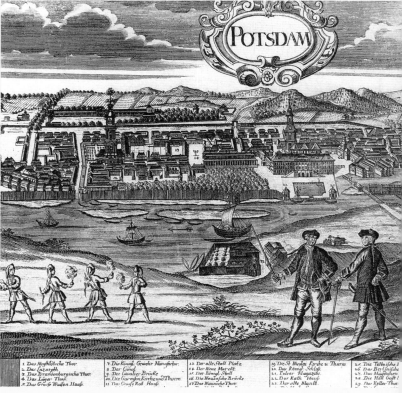

2

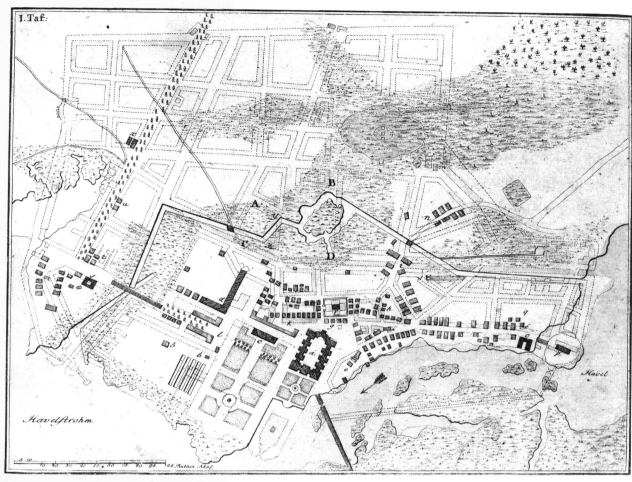

1 Bereits um 1955 hatte die DDR den Wiederaufbau des bürgerlichen Potsdam, hier in der Wilhelm-Staab-Straße, in Angriff genommen.

The GDR started to rebuild civilian Potsdam, here in Wilhelm-Staab-Strasse already around 1955.

2 Der Weg von der Langen Brücke in die Stadt hinein wurde von den Kolonnaden und dem Stadtschloß zum Alten Markt gelenkt; Aufnahme um 1940.

The way from the Lange Brücke into town led via the Kolonnaden and the Stadtschloss to the Old Market; photograph c. 1940.

3 Die herausragende Lage des Stadtschlosses am Wasser läßt die einstige Pracht der preußischen Residenzstadt Potsdam erahnen; hier um 1912 gesehen.

The Stadtschloss's outstanding site by the water gives a sense of the former glory of the Prussian monarchs' residence town; seen here in about 1912.

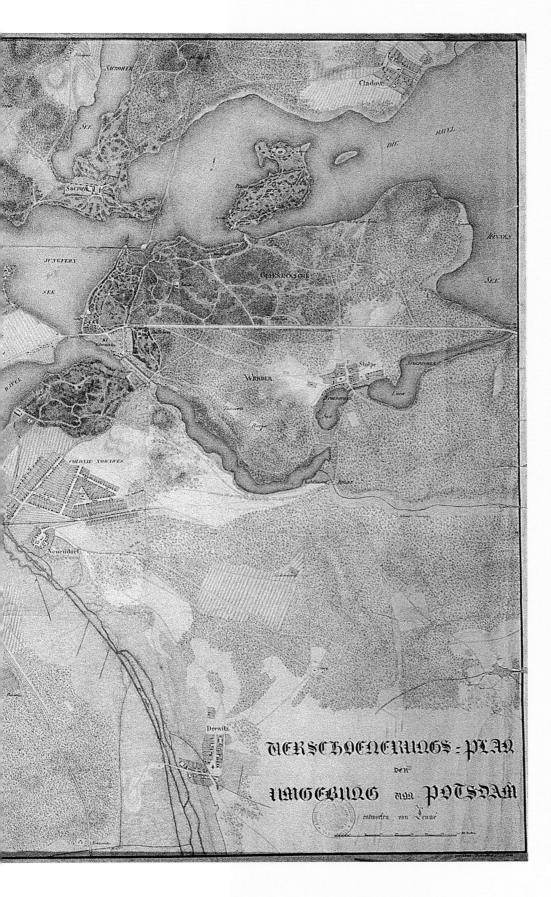

Der „Verschoenerungs-Plan der Umgebung von Potsdam entworfen von Lenné", 1833 von Gerh. Koerber gezeichnet, gilt als der gartenkünstlerische Ursprung der Stadt und Landschaft integrierenden „Kulturlandschaft".

The "Beautification plan for the Environs of Potsdam designed by Lenné", drawn by Gerh. Koerber in 1833 is the horticultural origin of the park landscape integrating town and countryside.

❶ In dem Schau- und Sichtungsgarten auf der Freundschaftsinsel, 1937 von Karl Foerster begründet, steht die Harmonie der Pflanzen im Vordergrund.

The specimen garden on Friendship Island was established by Karl Foerster in 1937, and concentrates on harmony in the plant world.

❷ Das südliche Torhaus wurde für die BUGA Potsdam 2001 in einstiger Gestalt neu errichtet.

The south gatehouse was restored to its original form for the National Horticultural Show.

❷

4

1

2

3

❶ Der Barockgarten, hier vor dem Neuen Palais in Potsdam, ordnet die Natur der Geometrie unter.

The Baroque garden, here in front of the Neues Palais in Potsdam, subordinates nature to geometry.

❷ Die Römischen Bäder im Park Sanssouci, eine „Welt en miniature", mit ihrem Biedermeiergarten.

The Roman Baths in the Sanssouci Park, a "world en miniature", with their Biedermeier garden.

❸ Der Senkgarten von Karl Foerster ist dem Respekt vor der Natur gewidmet.

Karl Foerster's sunken garden is dedicated to showing his respect for nature.

❹ Die domestizierte Landschaft der Gegenwart zwischen den Polen Kunst und Lebensraum.

The contemporary domesticated landscape, between the poles of art and biotope.

blühende Sträucher   Staudenstreifen

Der Park im Bornstedter Feld
The Park in the Bornstedter Feld

Der Park im Bornstedter Feld

Der sechzig Hektar große Park im Bornstedter Feld verbindet neue Wohnquartiere, Gewerbe- und Dienstleistungsstandorte und eine Fachhochschule in Neubauten und sanierten Kasernen inmitten einer insgesamt dreihundert Hektar großen städtischen Konversionsfläche, die direkt an die Innenstadt anschließt. Mit den geplanten und teils bereits fertiggestellten rund 7.500 Wohnungen im Geschoßwohnungsbau, in Stadtvillen und in Reihenhäusern ist das für 17.500 Einwohner sowie 5.000 Arbeitsplätze in Handel, Dienstleistung, Gewerbe und Forschung ausgelegte Bornstedter Feld das größte Stadtentwicklungsvorhaben Potsdams. Der Park inmitten vier neuer Quartiere wird nach seiner Nutzung als Park der Bundesgartenschau 2001 zum zentral gelegenen Stadtpark für dieses städtebauliche Entwicklungsvorhaben. Zugleich bildet der Park ein Scharnier, ein bisher fehlendes Verbindungsstück der historischen Gärten. Er leitet von Sanssouci und Ruinenberg über in die Lennésche Feldflur, zur russischen Siedlung Alexandrowka und zum Pfingstberg, von dem aus der schönste Sichtfächer den Blick auf alle historischen Schlösser und Parks der Potsdamer Kulturlandschaft freigibt. Nun auch auf den neuen Park im Bornstedter Feld.

Die Landschaftsarchitektur in Potsdam ist nicht bei Lenné stehengeblieben. Sichtbar im Park im Bornstedter Feld, dessen Konzeption die Landschaftsarchitekten Latz + Partner, Ampertshausen bei München, entwarfen, sind Elemente des Volksparks ebenso wie Zitate der Lennéschen Kulturlandschaft. Noch zu Lennés Zeiten gepflanzte Eichen der Viereckremise bilden den nördlichen Abschluß des Parks.

Peter Latz vertritt die Meinung, daß der Park der Gegenwart keine zu stark fixierten Nutzungsangebote machen darf – zu schnell wechseln die Ansprüche und Moden der Parknutzung. Ein Park aber soll dauerhaft funktionieren und überzeugen und darf daher Nutzungen nicht durch eine Ortszuweisung einschränken. Deshalb dominieren Wiesenflächen den Park. Gefaßt sind diese im Osten und Westen – also jeweils im Übergang zu neuen Stadtquartieren, die entlang des Parks mittels einer Parkrandstraße erschlossen werden – von bis zu fünfzig Meter breiten „Baumhallen". Durch die Baumhallen verläuft ein sandfarbener Asphaltweg rund um den Park. Der speziell gemischte Asphalt harmoniert in seiner Farbe mit den umliegenden Flächen, die als wassergebundene Wegedecke angelegt sind.

Das Motiv der Baumhallen und der als vier Kilometer langer Rundweg konzipierte „Schlechtwetterweg" halten den Park nicht nur optisch, sondern auch funktional zusammen. Der Weg bündelt die Besucherströme. Nach der Gartenschausaison ist dieser Weg auch als Radweg oder Skatebahn geeignet. Gerade deshalb werden die zu Fuß gehenden Besucher nicht streng auf diesem Weg gehalten, sondern sie können sich vom Rundweg aus den Park individuell erschließen. Die wassergebundene Wegedecke begleitet den Asphaltweg auf beiden Seiten. So entstehen weite Flächen unter Bäumen, die im Sinne der Idee des modernen Volksparks vielfältig nutzbar sind. Die Landschaftsarchitekten schaffen ein Angebot, das bei nur wenigen Besuchern im Park ebenso funktioniert wie bei großen Mengen an Gästen. Auf der wassergebundenen Decke sind temporäre Angebote vom Eisverkäufer bis zur Theatergruppe jederzeit denkbar.

Den Anforderungen an den Entwurf eines neuen Parks in historischer Kulturlandschaft wurde in einer Sichtraumanalyse als eigenständigem Planungsschritt Rechnung getragen. Aus den Aufgaben und Erfolgen der Gartendenkmalpflege der letzten Jahrzehnte hatte man gelernt, daß Sichtachsen im Laufe der Zeit zuwachsen, daß regelmäßiger Schnitt und Pflege die besten Maßnahmen zum Erhalt eines Parks sind und daß man auf diese Aspekte schon bei der Planung eines Parks Rücksicht nehmen kann. Also wurde festgelegt, wie hoch Gebäude im Park, vor allem das Gebäude der „Biosphäre Potsdam", aufragen dürfen, um selbst zum Blickpunkt zu werden, aber den Blick auf Ruinen- und Pfingstberg nicht zu verstellen. Ebenso sorgfältig analysierte man die Position neu zu pflanzender Bäume. Teils wurden bewußt Bäume gesetzt, so die blütenreichen Zierobstgehölze im südlichen Park, die den Blick auf den Ruinenberg öffnen, indem sie von einer problematisch situierten Wohnbebauung aus den frühen achtziger Jahren ablenken. Inmitten dieses Obsthains findet der aufmerksame Besucher eine aufgebrochene Betonfläche, die Latz + Partner als eine Spur der militärischen Nutzung in den neuen Park hinübergerettet haben.

Der speziell gesetzte Vegetationsschleier ist ebenso Ergebnis der Sichtraumanalyse wie freigelassene Sichtachsen anderorts. Vor allem aber hat man das Spiel mit Blicken inszeniert, indem man im Gelände vorhandene Wälle erhielt, über die heute Wege führen. Der Wechsel des Betrachtungsstandpunkts ist heute wortwörtlich der Höhepunkt des Gangs durch den Park. Die Wälle sind über Brücken und Stege verbunden und bieten vielfältige Blicke auf die nähere und weitere Umgebung.

Die Wälle sind ein Verweis auf die militärische Geschichte des Geländes. Sie wurden nach dem Zweiten Weltkrieg von den sowjetischen Alliierten auf dem jahrhundertealten Militärareal angelegt und sind durch eine eigenartige und unerklärliche Geometrie ihrer Lage und Form zu einer spannungsreichen Besonderheit des Parks geworden. Zu Zeiten Preußens war das Bornstedter Feld als ein von Kasernen umstellter Exerzierplatz so eben gestaltet, daß Anfang des zwanzigsten Jahrhunderts dort erste Flugversuche stattfinden konnten. Nach 1945 aber verschwand das Areal für Jahrzehnte fast vollständig aus dem öffentlichen Gedächtnis, so daß bis heute nur vermutet werden kann, daß die Wälle als Sichtschutz für die Tarnung militärischen Geräts angelegt wurden.

Erhaltung und Nutzung der Wälle gehen auf den im Frühjahr 1997 entschiedenen landschaftsplanerisch-städtebaulichen Ideenwettbewerb zurück, in dem der Entwurf des Büros Latz + Partner mit Hegger - Hegger - Schleiff Planer + Architekten, Kassel, und Jourda & Perraudin, Architekten, Lyon, mit dem ersten Preis ausgezeichnet wurde. Als einziger der Wettbewerbsteilnehmer erkannte Latz das Potential der Wälle und integrierte sie im Sinne seiner Philosophie des Respekts vor dem Vorgefundenen in den Entwurf.

Für den neuen Park sind die Wälle als Mittelpunkt und Identifikationsmotiv von herausragender Bedeutung. Denn sie bieten auf der ansonsten wenig bewegten Fläche eine spannungsreiche Höhenentwicklung. In einem gesondert ausgelobten Wettbewerb entwarf das Kölner Architekturbüro Dietrich, Fritzen, Löf einfache Brücken aus Cortenstahl mit einer eigenwilligen, rostroten Patina. Die Trogbrücken führen über die Wälle hinweg und lassen die Besucher auf den Wallkronen selbst, in die die Brückenelemente eingelassen wurden, über und zugleich durch die Wälle laufen.

Das größte der Wallrechtecke ist für große Veranstaltungen sowie für Sport und Spielangebote vorgesehen. Zum Thema Sport und Spiel im Park wurde ein eigenes Symposium durchgeführt, das den Charakter eines zeitgemäßen Volksparks definieren half. In das zentrale Wallkarree ist deshalb sowohl eine überdachte, multifunktionale Sportfläche, die zugleich als Bühne genutzt werden kann, integriert als auch ein großzügiger Skatebereich, der von den Gießener Landschaftsarchitekten Sommerlad Haase Kuhli in Zusammenarbeit mit Deutschlands „Skatepapst" Titus Dittmann konzipiert wurde. Südlich schließt der Spielwall für kleine und für Kinder mittleren Alters an (Entwurf: Büro Schirmer, Berlin). Entstanden ist eine vielfältige Wasserspiel

landschaft, die das Element Wasser in den Park auf dem Bornstedter Feld holt. Ein Café für Eltern und Kinder (Entwurf: Rolf Gnädinger, Architekt, Berlin) ist dort als dauerhaftes Gastronomieangebot in einen Wall integriert.

Die konkrete Planung der Wallareale übernahm das Büro Sommerlad Haase Kuhli. Die fotogenen und mit ihrem Duft lockenden Lavendelpflanzungen an einem der Wälle wurden von ihnen ebenso entwickelt wie die Verwendung von wildem Wein an den Außen- sowie von Rasen an den Innenhängen. Der Wein harmoniert in der Herbstfärbung hervorragend mit dem Cortenstahl der Brücken. Die Rasenhänge und -bermen laden zum Lagern ein – Landschaftstribünen quasi.

Wie einen Kragen legten Sommerlad Haase Kuhli die Schaupflanzungen der Rosen um die Wälle, jeweils eine Farbe und ein Thema dominieren die einzelnen Rosenfelder. Im Mittelpunkt der Wälle lockt das „Wallkreuz", ein Platz mit variablen Wasserspielen als zeitgemäß umgesetztes – und bespielbares – Motiv historischer Parkanlagen. Der lange Wassergraben mit den Irispflanzungen hat zugleich stadtökologische Funktion als Überlaufbecken für die Versickerung des Regenwassers, das in den benachbarten Stadtquartieren in Mulden und Rigolen gesammelt wird.

Das Motiv der Wälle inspirierte auch die Architekten der Biosphäre Potsdam. Regine Leibinger und Frank Barkow entwarfen in Zusammenarbeit mit den Landschaftsarchitekten Büro Kiefer, alle Berlin, ein außergewöhnliches Hallengebäude, das östlich an das Areal der Wälle anschließt. Das Dach dieser neuen Halle, die 2001 die Blumenschauen der BUGA zeigen und ab 2002 als ein Edutainment-Center zum Thema „Naturerlebnislandschaft Regenwald" genutzt wird, ist zu großen Teilen verglast. Es ist auf Wälle aufgelagert – ein landschaftliches Bauwerk. Der große, mit Schiefer belegte westliche Vorplatz mit Wassertisch und verschiebbaren Blumenkübeln in Stahl setzt sich auch im Gebäude fort. Außen- und Innenraum verlieren ihren trennenden Unterschied. Der Bau umhüllt Pflanzen, die andere Klimabedingungen benötigen. Er fällt im Park deshalb auf, aber nicht aus dem Park heraus. „Hinter dem Sichtbaren muß immer noch ein anderes Erreichbares durchblicken oder sich doch ahnen lassen, und die weiteste Ferne darf uns nicht verschlossen bleiben", schrieb Lenné 1826. Die Biosphäre überträgt diese Regel der Parkanlage in die heutige Architektur.

Weitere Blickfänger im Park sind die Staudentableaus, die bis zu zwei Meter aus dem Boden herausragen. Passend zu fränkischem und thüringischem Muschelkalk – neben Beton und sandfarbenem Asphalt drittes Leitmaterial im Park –, aus dem die Wallfüße und auch die Tableaus aufge mauert wurden, wählten die Gestalter der Pflanzungen, Christian Meyer und Christine Orel, auf Vorschlag der Landschaftsarchitekten als Leitmotiv grau- und silberlaubige Stauden aus, die farblich hervorragend mit dem Muschelkalk korrespondieren.

Die Staudenpflanzungen leiten über in den nördlichen Remisenpark. Dort wird mit sparsamen gestalterischen Mitteln an die Lennésche Feldflur angeknüpft. Eine noch vorhandene Eichenpflanzung im Quadrat – sie diente in den Planungen Lennés als „Remise", also als Unterstand und Schattenspender für das Vieh – wurde zum Namensgeber dieses Bereichs des Parks im Bornstedter Feld. Der Entwurf der Planungsgemeinschaft Remisenpark Potsdam der AG Freiraum Dittus und Böhringer mit Pit Müller, Freiburg, betont diese Remise durch ein quadratisches Holzdeck und untermalt ansonsten die Raumwirkung der vorhandenen Situation durch eine leichte Rasenmulde sowie seitliche Abpflanzungen mit Hecken, Stauden und Bäumen. Ein mit Platanen bepflanzter Platz leitet in das benachbarte Wohnquartier über, die Wegeführung aus dem südlichen Park wird fortgesetzt. Betonelemente laden zum Ausruhen ein. Schlicht, schön und unspektakulär bleibt der Park auch dort, wo er sich nach einer Engstelle im städtebaulichen Umfeld wieder aufweitet, ein Ergebnis der Volksparkidee.

Selbstverständlich ist der Park im Bornstedter Feld kein Volkspark der Wende zum 20. Jahrhundert, sondern ein Park mit den Intentionen der Gegenwart. Sein Charakteristikum aber, und da lehnt sich der Park im Bornstedter Feld deutlich an die Gestaltung der traditionellen Volksparks an, ist die Flexibilität der Nutzungsmöglichkeiten. Deshalb sah der Entwurf im wesentlichen vielfältig und flexibel nutzbare Wiesenflächen vor, auf denen jegliche Art von Lagern, Durchstreifen, Spielen, Toben möglich ist. Die großen, multifunktionalen Wiesenflächen sind besonders im südlichen Teil des Parks von Latz + Partner als Großer und Kleiner Wiesenpark beispielhaft im Sinne des Entwurfs umgesetzt worden. Die Wiesen werden teils als Langgraswiesen nur zwei Mal jährlich gemäht, im Zentrum des südlichen Parkabschnitts aber so häufig, daß Fußballspiel oder Drachensteigen möglich sind.

Orientierung im Park geben nicht unterschiedlich markierte Funktionsräume, sondern Orientierung gibt die einfache Struktur aus Baumhallen, Wiesenflächen und wieder Baumhallen. Die westlich und östlich gelegenen Baumkorridore sind in sich untergliedert, indem immer wieder Baumpakete gepflanzt wurden, die in ihrer Mitte aus höherwüchsigen Arten und Exemplaren bestehen und an ihren Rändern durch niedrigere Bäume abgestuft werden.

Für die Baumhallen verwendet Latz neben den standort-

typischen Leitbäumen Kiefer und Eiche bewußt eine Vielzahl an Baumarten, wobei eine Baumhalle jeweils von einer Baumart dominiert wird. Der Effekt des Arboretums, der durch die Vielfalt der Baumarten von großblättrigen Kastanien bis zu fiederblättrigen Robinien entsteht, ist gewünscht, denn Latz ist der Überzeugung, daß neugierige Besucher in einem Volkspark der Gegenwart auch einiges über Arten- und Wuchsvielfalt der Bäume lernen möchten. Die eingestreuten Nadelbäume sichern dem Park auch im Winter ein attraktives grünes Kleid.

Einen besonderen Rückzugsraum bildet der Waldpark im Osten des Parks im Bornstedter Feld. Das niederländische Bureau B + B inszenierte die Fläche, die in Potsdam als „Großer Schragen" bekannt ist, als einen ökologisch sensiblen, auf die Ruderalvegetation mit altem Eichen- und Pappelbestand besonders eingehenden Parkbereich. Der Waldpark wirkt als Ruheraum. Nur wenige neue, dafür betont artifizielle Elemente, die der niederländischen Gartenkunsttradition des einst wegen seiner Naturferne gescholtenen geometrischen, bunten und aus Materialien wie Porzellan, Muscheln und Glas gestalteten Ziergartens entlehnt sind, kontrastieren die sichtbaren Sukzessionsstadien im Waldpark – etwa pilzförmige Sitzsteine aus Beton, die frei im Raum verteilt sind. Meterhohe Betonelemente, dunkelrot eingefärbt, laden zum Spiel auf einer Vielzahl unterschiedlich abenteuerlicher Rutschen ein. Zu erklimmende Außenwände der Beton-„Terminals" grenzen Räume ab. Einer davon wird zum Beachvolleyballplatz. Jogger und Spaziergänger können den Waldpark auf mit Glasbruch bestreuten, grünbunt schimmernden Trampelpfaden durchstreifen. Diese „Spuren" sind nachts durch kleine Solarleuchten markiert, Spuren zivilisatorischer Zukunft in der inszenierten Wildnis. Die alten Baumbestände werden erhalten, selbst wenn sie von Misteln dicht besetzt zusammenzubrechen drohen. Weite Ringe aus Leseholz um die Altbäume herum schaffen nicht zu betretende, sich selbst überlassene Zonen, so daß kein Besucher von herabfallenden Ästen verletzt werden kann. Die ehemals in Bodensenken angelegten „Panzer-Verstecke" sind im Waldpark als Schaufläche für Rhododendren zivilisiert worden.

Die bildende Kunst ergänzt die gärtnerische Schöpfung. Zum Beispiel das Kunstwerk Camofields der Potsdamer Künstlergruppe BergWerk, bei dem Sitzgelegenheiten, in Tarnstoffen der Armeen aus aller Welt gekleidet, im Waldpark wie im gesamten Park im Bornstedter Feld verteilt werden. Dieses Kunstwerk wurde in einem eigenständigen künstlerischen Wettbewerb zum Thema „Tarnung und Enttarnung" ausgewählt und mit Unterstützung der Bundeswehr realisiert, die Kontakt zu Armeen anderer Nationen aufnahm und um Tarnmuster bat. Diese unterscheiden sich nämlich von Land zu Land, von Armee zu Armee, je nach ortstypischer Erdoberfläche und Vegetation von dschungelgrün bis wüstengelb oder polarweiß.

Das Camofields-Kunstwerk erinnert in besonderer Weise an die militärische Vergangenheit des Parkareals, während das „K" des Berliner Künstlers Fritz Balthaus ironisch mit der Kunst im öffentlichen Raum spielt. In Übertragung des Signets für Kunstwerke in einem Lageplan für den BUGA-Park Magdeburg, nämlich ein schwarzes „K" auf weißem Grund, baute Balthaus eine 12,5 mal 12,5 Meter große, weiß gestrichene Betonfläche an einem der schönsten Orte im Waldpark, auf die er ein „K" aus schwarzem Polyurethan aufbringt. Kunstwerk eben. Schwarz auf weiß. Der Ort lädt zur Diskussion über das Wesen der Kunst ein.

Mit der Freizeit- und Sportleidenschaft spielt dagegen das „Basketballfeld" der Künstler inges idee, Berlin. Das ebenfalls im Waldpark gelegene Sportfeld ist der vorgefundenen Topographie angepaßt – roter Kunststoffbelag mit allen Markierungen und mit Körben, aber nicht eben. Neue Sporterfahrungen durch verspringende Bälle sind zu erwarten.

Mit den an Filmkulissen erinnernden Fassaden von Andreas Siekmann, Berlin, und dem zu einem Spiegelkabinett der Künstlerin Annette Wehrmann, Hamburg, umgewidmeten ehemaligen Wachturm aus der Zeit der militärischen Nutzung werden weitere künstlerische Akzente im Park gesetzt. Statt die Umgebung zu überwachen, wird der Besucher im Wachturm auf sich selbst zurückgeworfen. Im Remisenpark läßt der Künstler Igor Sacharow-Ross, Köln, das ehemalige Schießhaus überwuchern und setzt sich so ebenfalls mit der militärischen Vergangenheit des Bornstedter Feldes auseinander.

So ist der Park im Bornstedter Feld die zeitgenössische Fortsetzung der Geschichte Potsdams und zugleich eine Antwort auf die Frage nach der Entwicklung dieser Stadt. Es sollte die Besucher nicht weiter verwirren, daß Teile des für die Bundesgartenschau angelegten Parks auf späteren Baufeldern entstehen, also nach 2001 bebaut werden; hier liegt eine besonders gelungene Verbindung von Ökonomie und Gartenkunst vor, können doch Erschließungstrassen und -wege nachgenutzt werden. Damit erhält Potsdam gleichzeitig neue Quartiere, einen neuen Park und ein neues Kulturangebot. Weniger darf eine Gartenschau in Potsdam nicht leisten.

The Park in the Bornstedter Feld

The Park im Bornstedter Feld (Park in the Bornstedter Feld) covers an area of sixty hectares and links new residential areas, commercial and service sites as well as a college accommodated in new buildings and refurbished barracks in the middle of a hundred hectare urban redevelopment area immediately adjacent to the city centre. The Bornstedter Feld is Potsdam's largest urban development project, with about 7,500 dwellings planned in apartment buildings, urban villas and terraced houses to accommodate 17,500 residents, and also offering 5,000 jobs in trade, services, commerce and research. The park in the middle of four new districts will be used for the 2001 National Horticultural Show, and will then become the central municipal park in this urban development project. At the same time, the park forms a pivotal link with the historical gardens that has so far been missing. It forms a transition from Sanssouci and Ruinenberg to Lenné's meadowland, the Russian Alexandrowska estate and the Pfingstberg, which provides a wonderful panoramic view of all the historical parks and gardens in Potsdam's developed landscape.

Landscape architecture in Potsdam did not come to a standstill with Lenné. The Park in the Bornstedter Feld was conceived by landscape architects Latz + Partner of Ampertshausen near Munich, and combines elements of the people's park with quotations from the landscape as developed by Lenné. The park is bordered on the north side by oaks planted in Lenné's time to form the square Remise – a thicket to provide shade for cattle.

Peter Latz thinks that a contemporary park should not be too rigid in the uses it offers – the demands and fashions relating to park use are changing far too quickly. But a park should work and convince in the long term, and thus should not restrict uses by allocating them a precise location. For this reason the park is dominated by areas of grass. On the east and west sides, in other words at the points of transition to new urban districts to which access is provided along the park by means of a road running along its edge, it is framed by "tree halls" up to fifty metres wide. A sand-coloured asphalt path runs round the park through the tree halls. The specially mixed asphalt harmonizes in colour with the surrounding areas that are laid out as a water-bound surface.

The motif of the tree halls and the "bad weather path", designed as a four kilometre route round the park, hold it together both visually and functionally. This path channels the streams of visitors. Once the horticultural show season is over it is also suitable for use as a cycle track, or for roller-skating and skateboarding. And for precisely this reason pedestrians are not too strictly confined to this path, but can also make individual forays into the park from the circular route. The water-bound surface runs on both sides of the asphalt path. This creates large areas under trees that can be used in a number of ways, in accordance with the idea of a modern people's park. The landscape architects are creating a range of possibilities that will work if there are not many visitors in the park or when there are huge crowds. Temporary facilities from ice-cream salesmen to theatre groups are conceivable on the water-bound surface.

The demands made on a design for a park in a historically cultivated and developed landscape were addressed in a visual analysis included as an independent design step. People had learned from the demands made on and successes achieved by historical garden preservation in recent decades that sightlines can become overgrown in the course of time, that regular cutting and care are the best measures for the upkeep of a park and that these aspects can be considered even when the park is at the planning stage. So a decision was taken about how high buildings in the park, particularly the Potsdam Biosphere, could be allowed to be in order to attract attention but not to spoil the view of the Ruinenberg and the Pfingstberg. The positions in which new trees were to be planted were also analysed very carefully. Some trees were placed for a particular purpose, like the decorative, heavy-flowering fruit trees in the southern part of the park which open up a view of the Ruinenberg by distracting attention from a problematically placed residential development dating from the early eighties. Attentive visitors will find a broken-up area of concrete in the middle of this grove of fruit trees. This was rescued by Latz + Partner as a reminder of the former military presence in the new park.

This specially placed veil of vegetation is as much a result of the visual analysis as are the sightlines left open elsewhere. Very special games with views have been played by retaining existing embankments on the site and by running paths along the top of them. Changing viewpoints are now literally the high point of a walk through the park. The "ramparts" are linked by bridges and walkways and offer a range of views in the immediate vicinity and further away.

The embankments are a reminder of the military history of the area. They were built after the Second World War by the Soviet Allies on this centuries-old military site, and have become an exciting special feature of the park because of the unique and inexplicable geometry of their position and form. In Prussian times the Bornstedter Feld was a parade ground surrounded by barracks, and so flat that early flying experiments were made from it in the early twentieth century. But after 1945 the site disappeared almost completely from the public memory for decades, so that today we can only assume that the embankments were intended as camouflage for military equipment.

The retention and use of the banks goes back to the landscape and urban development competition in which the first prize was won by the office of Latz + Partner with Hegger-Hegger-Schleiff Planer + Architekten of Kassel and Jourda & Perraudin, architects, of Lyon. Latz was the only competition entrant to recognize the potential of the "ramparts", making them an integral part of the design in the spirit of his philosophy that his creative work should respect what is found on a site.

The "ramparts" are of outstanding importance for the new park, providing both a focal point and a means of identification, as they offer an exciting height difference on a site that is otherwise dead in this respect. In a separate competition, the Cologne architects' office of Dietrich, Fritzen, Löf designed simple bridges in Corten steel with an unusual rust-red patina. These trough bridges run beyond the "ramparts", and allow visitors to walk over and at the same time through the banks on the tops of the walls themselves, into which the bridge elements have been inserted.

The largest of the rectangles contained by the "ramparts" is intended for major events, sports fixtures and games. A symposium held on the subject of sport and games in the park helped to define the character of a contemporary people's park. Thus the central area within the banks contains a roofed, multi-functional sports field that can double as a stage, and also a generous skateboarding area, the funwall, designed by the Giessen landscape architects Sommerlad Haase Kuhli, working with Germany's skateboarding authority Titus Dittmann. On the south side is the "play rampart" for small and middle-aged children (designed by Büro Schirmer, Berlin). This involves a diverse landscape of water features, introducing water as an element into the Park in the Bornstedter Feld. A café for parents and children (design: Rolf Gnädinger, architect, Berlin) is built into one of the embankments as a permanent feature.

Detailed planning for the embankment sites by Sommerlad Haase Kuhli includes photogenic and fragrant lavender plantations and the use of wild vines on the outer slopes and lawns on the inner slopes. The autumn colours of the vines harmonize perfectly with the Corten steel of the bridges. The sloping lawns and berms invite people to lie down – almost like grandstands in the landscape.

Sommerlad Haase Kuhli laid the show plantations of roses around the embankments like a collar, and each of the floral areas is dominated by a colour and a theme. The central point of the banks is the "rampart cross", a square with variable water features as a motif borrowed from historic parks, implemented for today – and available to play on. The long moat planted with iris also functions as a piece of urban ecology, as an overflow basin from which rainwater collected in troughs and trenches in the neighbouring districts of the town can infiltrate.

The "rampart" theme also inspired the architects of the Potsdam Biosphere. Regine Leibinger and Frank Barkow, working with Büro Kiefer landscape architects, all of Berlin, designed an extraordinary hall building on the south side of the embankment area. The hall will be used in 2001 for the flower shows, then from 2002 as an edutainment centre on the theme of "Rain Forest as a Natural Adventure Landscape". The roof of the hall is supported by embankments – a landscape building. The large, slate-paved west forecourt with water-table and movable steel flower tubs is continued inside the building. Interior and exterior space are no longer clearly divided. The building contains plants that need different climatic conditions. It is a striking feature of the park, but also remains a part of the park. "Something that is different yet accessible must always be glimpsed through what is visible, or at least be sensed as a presence, and even the farthest distance must not remain closed to us", wrote Lenné in 1826. The Biosphere applies this rule for parks to contemporary architecture.

The herbaceous tableaux, which rise up to two metres out of the ground, are another eye-catching feature of the park. In keeping with the Franconian and Thuringian shell limestone – the third principal material in the park alongside concrete and sandy-coloured asphalt – from which both the wall bases and the raised masonry for the tableaux were constructed, the planting designers, Christian Meyer and Christine Orel, chose grey- and silver-leaved herbaceous perennials, which tone in perfectly with the stone.

The herbaceous planting forms a transition to the Remisenpark (Shelter Park) in the north. Here economical design approaches are used to link up with Lenné's Meadowland. A square oak plantation has survived – it served as a shelter for cattle, in Lenné's plans –, and gave its name to this part of the Park in the Bornstedter Feld. The design by the Remisenpark Potsdam Planning Association of Freiraum Dittus und Böhringer with Pit Müller, Freiburg, emphasizes this shelter with a square timber deck and also accompanies the spatial effect made by the existing situation with a shallow grassy dip and side-planting with hedges, herbaceous plants and trees. A square planted with plane trees forms the transition to the adjacent residential area, and the pathways from the southern part of the park are continued. Concrete elements invite visitors to sit down and rest. The park remains simple, beautiful and unspectacular even at the point where it broadens out again after a bottleneck in the urban surroundings – an achievement for the people's park idea.

Of course the Park in the Bornstedter Feld is not a people's park of the kind that emerged in the late 19th and early 20th century, but a park with contemporary intentions. However, the park does clearly borrow from the traditional people's park in its chief characteristic, which is the flexibility of the uses it offers. For this reason the design provided a wide range of grassy areas that can be used flexibly, where people can lie down, wander around, play or tear about. These large, multifunctional grassy areas have been implemented in the spirit of the design in the southern part of Latz + Partner's park in the form of the Grosser und Kleiner Wiesenpark (Large and Small Meadow Parks). Part of the area has the grass left long – it is mown only twice per year – but in the centre of the southern section of the park it is mown frequently enough for it to be possible to play football or fly kites.

Visitors do not find their way around the park by differently marked functional areas, but by the simple structure of tree halls, meadow areas and then more tree halls. The tree corridors to the east and west have their own substructure provided by the repeated planting of clumps of trees made up of taller species and specimens in the centre, working down to lower trees on the edges.

For the tree halls Latz uses pine and oak, which are indigenous to the area, but also deliberately adds a number of species, with each tree hall dominated by a particular kind of tree. The arboretum effect given by the wide range of trees from broad-leaved chestnut to narrow-leaved robinia is as Latz wished, as he felt that curious visitors to a contemporary people's park would also like to learn something about different species of tree and the way they grow. A scattering of conifers ensures that the park is attractively clad in green even in the winter.

The Waldpark (Wooded Park) in the eastern area of the Park in the Bornstedter Feld offers a specially secluded place. The Dutch Bureau B + B presented this area, which is known in Potsdam as the "Grosser Schragen", as an ecologically sensitive piece of parkland paying particular attention to ruderal vegetation with an existing stock of old oak and poplar. The Waldpark conveys the impression of an area devoted to peace and quiet. Only a few new and emphatically artificial elements, borrowed from the Dutch horticultural tradition of geometrical, colourful decorative gardens created from materials like porcelain, shells and glass, and once criticized for being unnatural, form a contrast with the vis-

ible stages of succession in the Waldpark – for example mushroom-shaped concrete benches spread freely around the space. Metre-high concrete elements, dyed dark red, invite people to play on slides offering various degrees of thrill. The outer walls of the concrete "terminals" separate spaces off. One of these forms a beach-volleyball court. Joggers and walkers make their way through the Waldpark on well-trodden paths strewn with treated glass waste, colourfully shimmering in green. At night these "tracks" are marked by little solar lamps, traces of a civilized future in a theatrically staged wilderness. The old-established trees are retained, even if they are so thick with mistletoe that they threaten to collapse. Wide circles of fallen wood around the old trees create no-entry zones that are left to themselves, so that visitors cannot be hurt by falling branches. The "tank traps" that used to be fitted in dips have been civilized in the Waldpark as rhododendron show areas.

Fine art complements the horticultural creations. These include the Camofields work of art by the group of Potsdam artists BergWerk, in which seats, covered in the camouflage fabrics used by armies from all over the world, are distributed around the Waldpark and the whole of the Park in the Bornstedter Feld. This work was chosen in an independent artistic competition on the subject of "Concealing and Revealing", and realized with the assistance of the German Army, who got in touch with armies from other countries and asked them to contribute camouflage patterns. These in fact differ from country to country, according to the local terrain and vegetation, from jungle green to desert yellow or polar white.

The Camofields work of art is especially reminiscent of the park site's military past, while Berlin artist Fritz Balthaus's "K" plays ironically with art in public places. By transforming the logo for art in a plan for the park of the National Horticultural Show in Magdeburg, a black "K" on a white ground, Balthaus constructed a large, white-painted area of concrete in one of the most beautiful locations in the Waldpark, and placed a black polyurethane "K" on top of it. A work of art, precisely. Black on white. This place will invite discussion about the nature of art.

In contrast with this, the Basketballfeld (Basketball Court) by the Berlin artists inges idee plays with the notion of being passionate about leisure and sport. This sports field, also in the Waldpark, adapts to the existing topography – it has a red plastic surface with the appropriate line-markings and baskets, but it is not flat. New sporting experiences with balls bouncing all over the place are anticipated. Façades by Andreas Siekmann, Berlin, and the former watch-tower from the period of military use, turned into a cabinet of mirrors by the Hamburg artist Annette Wehrmann, are reminiscent of film sets and provide further artistic landmarks in the park. Instead of keeping watch over the surrounding area, visitors to the watch-tower are thrown back on their own resources. In the Remisenpark the artist Igor Sacharow-Ross, Cologne, has allowed the former shooting gallery to become overgrown, thus addressing the Bornstedter Feld's military past.

Thus the Park in the Bornstedter Feld is a contemporary continuation of Potsdam's history and at the same time a response to the question about how this town should develop in future. Visitors should not be confused by the fact that parts of the park are on land designated for building after 2001; this is a particularly successful combination of economics and horticulture, as it will be possible to re-use the access roads and paths after the event. Thus Potsdam will be acquiring new districts, a new park and new cultural facilities, all at the same time. A horticultural show in Potsdam should aspire to achieve no less.

❶ Park im Bornstedter Feld: Der Übersichtsplan zeigt die zentrale Wallandschaft mit der Biosphäre. Das Gerüst des Parks bildet eine Struktur aus Baumhallen, Wiesenflächen und wieder Baumhallen. Ein 4 km langer Rundweg erschließt den Park.

Park in the Bornstedter Feld: the outline plan shows the central "rampart" area and the Biosphere. The park is built on a framework of tree halls, meadows, then again tree halls. Access to the park is provided by a circular path four kilometers long.

❷ Blick über das Gelände nach Westen. Im Vordergrund die Biosphäre.

View of the site looking west. The Biosphere is in the foreground.

1

1 Staudentableaus nach dem Entwurf der Landschaftsarchitekten
Sommerlad Haase Kuhli. Als Leitmotiv wurden grau- und silberlaubige Stauden ausgesucht, die
farblich hervorragend mit dem
Muschelkalk korrespondieren.

**Herbaceous tableaux designed by
landscape architects Sommerlad
Haase Kuhli. Herbaceous plants
with grey and silver foliage were
selected as a leitmotif, and they
make an outstanding colour contrast with the shell limestone.**

2 Einer der Wälle mit duftenden
Lavendelpflanzungen.

**One of the "ramparts" planted with
fragrant lavender.**

3 Wie einen Kragen legen Sommerlad
Haase Kuhli die Rosenpflanzungen
um die Wälle. Die Form der einzelnen Pflanzungen soll selbst an eine
Blüte erinnern.

**Sommerlad Haase Kuhli have
planted roses around the "ramparts"
like collars. The shapes of the
various plantings are supposed to
evoke a blossom.**

2

❸

②

①

③

① Die Dekadengärten nach einem Konzept des Büros Isterling zeigen Gartenmoden der 50er, 60er, 70er 80er und 90er Jahre. Unten die 50er Jahre.

The Decade Gardens are based on an idea by the Isterling office, and show garden fashions in the 50s, 60s, 70s, 80s and 90s. Below: the 50s.

② Auf zukünftigen Baufeldern werden vorübergehend nachwachsende Rohstoffe gezeigt.

Renewable raw material appear in temporary exhibitions on future building sites.

③ Der Spielplatz im Remisenpark führt in die Baumkronen.

The playground in Shelter Park leads up into the tops of the trees.

④ Im Remisenpark mit seinem alten Baumbestand wird mit sparsamen gestalterischen Mitteln an die Lennésche Gestaltung angeknüpft. Entwurf der Arbeitsgemeinschaft Remisenpark Potsdam.

Minimal design measures are used to link the Shelter Park and its old trees with Lenné's design. Design by the Arbeitsgemeinschaft Remisenpark Potsdam.

❶ Skulpturale Versickerungsspiralen legten Latz + Partner auf dem Parkgelände an.

Latz + Partner placed sculptural infiltration spirals in the park.

❷ Im Großen Wiesenpark kontrastieren Baumhallen und weite Flächen.

Tree halls and wide-open spaces form a contrast in the Large Meadow Park.

❸ Jede Baumhalle wird von einer bestimmten Baumart dominiert. So entsteht der Effekt eines Arboretums.

Each tree hall is dominated by a particular species, giving the effect of an arboretum.

❹ Der Obsthain als südlicher Abschluß des Parks.

The fruit grove marks the southern end of the park.

❶

❸

❹

❶ Einen Rückzugs- und Ruheraum
bildet der Waldpark. Das niederländische Bureau B+B inszenierte die
Fläche als einen ökologisch sensiblen, auf die Ruderalvegetation mit
altem Eichen- und Pappelbestand
eingehenden Parkbereich.

The Wooded Park offers peace and
quiet. The Dutch Bureau B+B presented the area as an ecologically
sensitive park, responding to the
ruderal vegetation and the stock of
old oaks and poplars.

❷ Große Betonskulpturen sind zugleich Spielplätze und Irritationen
inmitten des Wildwuchses.

Large concrete sculptures are playgrounds and also disturb the pattern
of wild growth.

❸ Wenige artifizielle Elemente kontrastieren mit den sichtbaren Sukzessionsstadien im Waldpark – zum
Beispiel pilzförmige Sitzsteine aus
Beton.

A small number of artificial elements provide a contrast with the
visible stages of biological succession in the Wooded Park – these
mushroom-shaped concrete seats,
for example.

❹ In ehemaligen „Panzertaschen"
werden heute Rhododendrenpflanzungen präsentiert.

Rhododendron plantations now
occupy the former "tank pockets".

1 Annette Wehrmann, Hamburg: „Der Turm".

Annette Wehrmann, Hamburg: "The Tower".

2 Igor Sacharow-Ross, Köln: „Der Zaun".

Igor Sacharow-Ross, Cologne: "The Fence".

❶ BergWerk, Potsdam: „Camofields".

BergWerk, Potsdam: "Camofields".

❷ Fritz Balthaus, Berlin: „K".

Fritz Balthaus, Berlin: "K".

❸ inges idee, Berlin:
„Das Basketballfeld".

**inges idee, Berlin:
"The Basketball Court".**

❹ Andreas Siekmann, Berlin:
„Hier baut die Firma Petit à Petit ".

**Andreas Siekmann, Berlin:
"Petit à Petit at work".**

❹

❶ Der Gestaltung der öffentlichen Freiräume im späteren Wohngebiet Bornstedter Feld wird große Bedeutung beigemessen. Ein Beispiel ist der Platz am „Tor zum Park" von Levin Monsigny, Berlin.

Great importance is attached to the design of the public open spaces in the future Bornstedter Feld residential area. The "Gateway to the Park" square by Levin Monsigny, Berlin, is an example of this.

❷ Bornstedter Feldflur: Aussichtspunkt am Birnenweg. Kleine Plattformen laden zum Sitzen ein und lassen den Blick in die weite Kulturlandschaft schweifen.

Bornstedter Feldflur: Birnenweg vantage point. Little platforms invite you to sit and let your eyes roam around the wide expanses of Potsdam's man-made landscape.

❸ Für den Park wurde Gartenmobilar neu entworfen.

New garden furniture was designed for the park.

❶

❷

3

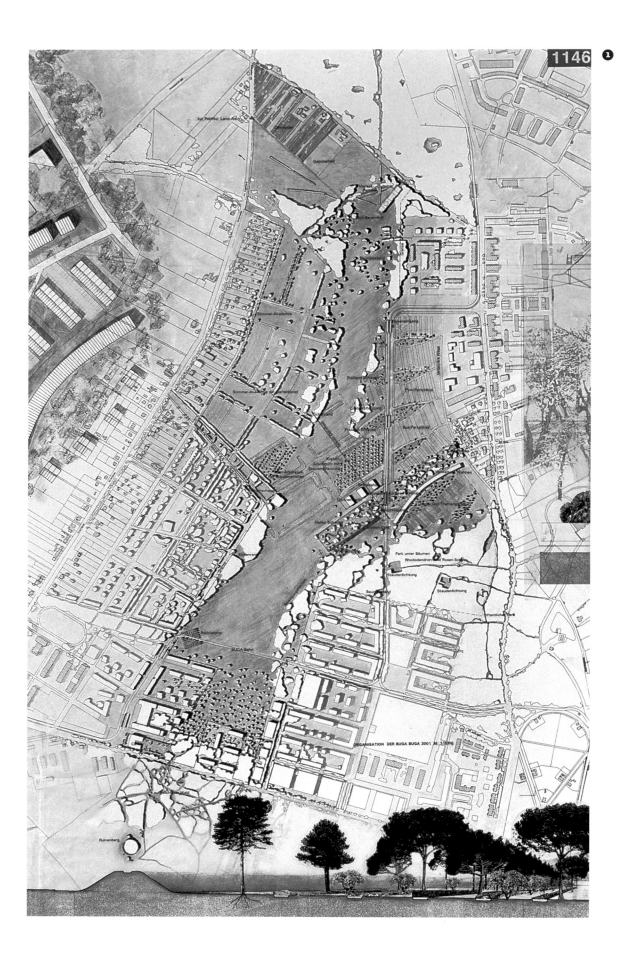

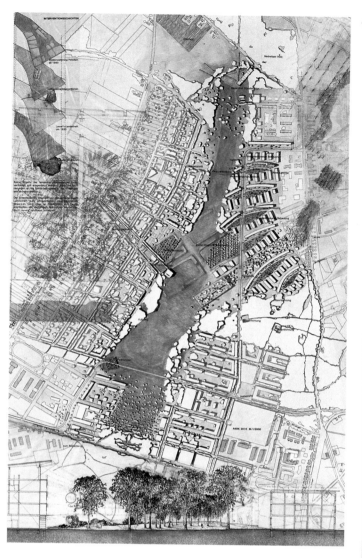

❶ Im Landschaftsplanerisch-Städtebaulichen Ideenwettbewerb 1997 wurde das Konzept von Latz + Partner, Kranzberg bei München, mit Jourda & Perraudin, Lyon, sowie Hegger-Hegger-Schleiff Planer + Architekten, Kassel, prämiert.

The concept submitted by Latz + Partner, Kranzberg near München, with Jourda & Perraudin, Lyon, and Hegger-Hegger-Schleiff Planer + Architekten, Kassel won in the 1997 landscape planning and urban development ideas competition.

❷ Die Wettbewerbsteilnehmer waren aufgefordert, den Park für die Bundesgartenschau 2001 zu entwerfen, aber auch ein integriertes Konzept für Park und Städtebau 2010 vorzulegen.

The competition entrants were invited to design the park for the National Horticultural Show 2001, but also to submit an integrated concept for the park and urban development in 2010.

❸ Der Entwurf des niederländischen Bureau B + B, Amsterdam für den Waldpark wurde nach dem ersten Wettbewerb entwickelt.

The Dutch Bureau B + B, Amsterdam design for the Wooded Park was developed after the first competition.

❶ Der innovative Wettbewerbsentwurf von Winy Maas, MVRDV, Rotterdam mit Hemprich + Tophof Architekten, Berlin, erhielt einen Ankauf. Elemente des Parks und des Städtebaus wechseln einander auf der gesamten Fläche ab.

The innovative competition design by Winy Maas, MVRDV, Rotterdam with Hemprich + Tophof Architekten, Berlin, achieved a mention. Urban and park elements alternate throughout the area.

❷ Bis 2010 entsteht in den Vorstellungen von MVRDV im Bornstedter Feld ein völlig neuartiger Stadttyp. Landschaft und Stadt stoßen nicht mehr aneinander, sondern lösen sich ineinander auf.

MVRDV's ideas would produce a completely new urban type in the Bornstedter Feld by 2010. Landscape and town no longer collide, but dissolve within each other.

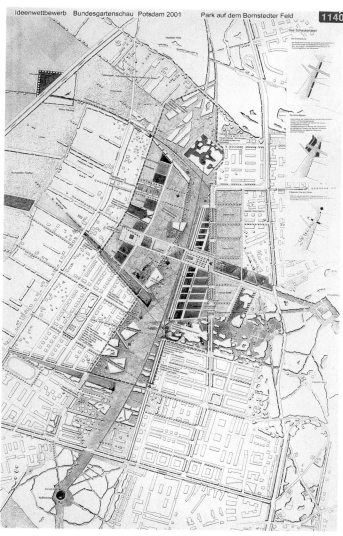

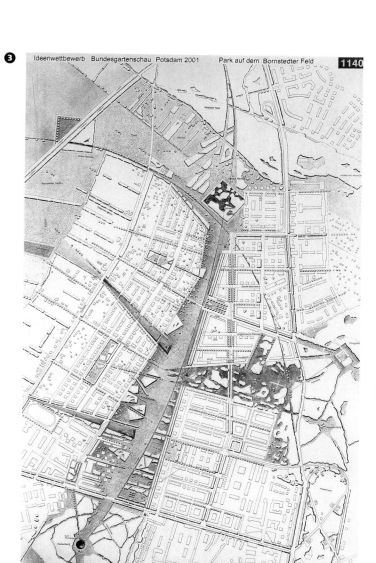

❸ Aus dem Wettbewerb wurde das Konzept für den Remisenpark übernommen. Für ihren Parkentwurf erhielten AG Freiraum, Freiburg, mit den Architekten Binkert und Melder, Freiburg, den 3. Preis.

The concept for the Shelter Park was adopted from the competition. AG Freiraum, Freiburg, with architects Binkert und Melder, Freiburg, were awarded the 3rd prize for their park design.

❹ Die Remise im Norden des Parks wird in diesem Vorschlag zum bestimmenden Elemente für Stadt und Freiraum. Städtebaulich wird ansonsten konventionelle Blockrandbebauung vorgeschlagen.

In this proposal the Remise (shelter for cattle) in the northern section of the park becomes the defining element for urban and open space. Otherwise, conventional block-edge development is proposed as an urban development measure.

Essay von **Peter Wilson**

Das epische Maß der Landschaft
Über die Biosphäre Potsdam

Vor etwa zehn Jahren zeichnete ich eine kleine Landschaftsskizze in mein Notizbuch. Es war zu der Zeit, als der Computer Einzug in die Architekturbüros hielt, um das Handzeichnen zu verdrängen – als die Bilder sich auf digitale Trajektorien begaben und der Text sich von der Tyrannei des Mechanischen losriß, um über jedwede Oberfläche zu treiben. Meine Skizze war nichts Besonderes – bis auf die Tatsache, daß sie bei Sonnenschein entstand und der Wind währenddessen am Papier riß. Die Landschaft war nicht Brandenburg, hätte es aber sein können. Eine dunkle Baumlinie verband linke und rechte Bildseite miteinander. Graue Farbe im oberen Blattbereich deutete atmosphärische Turbulenzen an. Ein flammengleiches Orange im dunklen Band der Bäume verwies auf eine bestimmte Phase im jährlichen Wachstumszyklus. Am rechten Bildrand lief eine handgeschriebene Wörterliste von oben nach unten: .....swivel tilt move persp yes hide no carpet off frame auto y draw plot three iso axo undump view type round advance zoom.....

Dieser inzwischen vertraute Menütyp weist heute nicht nur den Rechner an, sondern auch unsere Augen. Unser Wahrnehmungsapparat, unsere „Sehweise", ist umprogrammiert worden. Ohne mit der Wimper zu zucken, akzeptieren wir heute, daß Text fliegen kann, daß zuvor distinkte Objekte sich zu jedweder Menge fremder Körper verformen können, daß der bevorzugte einzigartige Blickwinkel der klassischen Perspektive durch eine neue Form von Image- und Informationsflux verdrängt worden ist. In der postdigitalen Wahrnehmung geht es um losgelöste Informationsbits, visuelle Fragmente, deren Sequenzen keine höhere Ordnung offenbaren und bei denen der Schockfaktor der Diskontinuität, mit dem der Surrealismus einst die Konvention herausforderte, nun seinerseits Konvention geworden ist. Der Status von Landschaft ist gegen diese radikale Neupositionierung nicht immun geblieben. Als Metapher liefert die „Landschaft" eine topographische Analogie zu neuen Datenfeldern. Diese Situation ruft nach einer reziproken postdigitalen Wiederherstellung der Möglichkeiten von Landschaft.

Ein charakteristischer Bezug zur Landschaft ist ein grundlegendes Attribut einer jeden Epoche. Der englische Landschaftsgärtner Humphrey Repton beschrieb das georgianische England treffend mit der Feststellung, „ein Gentleman, und um wieviel mehr eine Gentlewoman, hätte fern der Gesellschaft keinen Blick aus dem Fenster denn auf sanft hügelige Rasenflächen und Parks geworfen". Einhundert Jahre später insistierte Adolf Loos, „ein Gentleman sieht nicht aus dem Fenster". Auch Lennés Potsdamer Landschaftsgärten gehörten zum charakteristischen Panorama des 19. Jahrhunderts; vermag eine Bundesgartenschau in Potsdam dasselbe für den gegenwärtigen Moment der Geschichte zu sein?

Wie beurteilen wir eine reale Landschaft, einen metrischen Raum, dessen topographische Dimensionen nach wie vor direkt erlebt, körperlich durchschritten werden? Wie setzen wir diesen gemessenen

Raum in Bezug zum topologischen Raum der Informationstechnologie, die das Konzept Landschaft für indeterminierte Felder aus Kontinuitäten und Relationen heranzieht?

Die zeitgenössische Feldtheorie gibt dem inneren Beziehungsgeflecht den Vorrang vor der Gesamtform. Im Gegensatz zu den Eigenschaften eines spezifischen Ortes ist ein Feld ein unspezifischer Zustand. Die zeitgenössische Feldtheorie bezieht auch dynamische räumliche Beziehungen mit ein: Vogelschwärme und ähnlich komplexe Phänomene lassen sich als quantifizierbare räumliche Matrix wiedergeben, was einen Paradigmenwechsel vom Statischen zum Fließenden darstellt. Aber was ist mit der Landschaft selbst? Soll nun auch sie, als Reaktion auf die Komplexität momentaner Bedingungen, in Wellen oszillieren, oder gewinnt sie neue Bedeutung als Hintergrund und Maß für die hyperaktiven Trajektorien?

HORIZONTAL VERTIKAL

Niederländische Feldtheorie in Form von wechselnden Anordnungen vielfältiger, doch in sich konsistenter Landschaftspakete ist im wesentlichen ein zweidimensionales Spiel. Die Niederlande sind ein flaches Land. Es ist ein Spiel aus kollagierten, sehr unterschiedlichen Dichtegraden – die Niederlande sind auch ein kleines Land. Dieses Spiel macht ganz wie unsere heutigen Medien außerdem wenig Unterschied zwischen dem Künstlichen und jeglicher Idee von Authentizität oder Natürlichkeit – die gebaute Polderlandschaft Hollands ist ein von Menschenhand gemachtes Artefakt. Der holländische EXPO-Pavillon in Hannover von MVRDV hat die der exzessiven Landaneignung innewohnenden politischen und wirtschaftlichen Schwierigkeiten durch Stapelung geschickt umgangen. Fünf aufeinander gestapelte Landschaften sind, der Logik des Big Mac folgend, besser als fünf eingeschossige Landschaften nebeneinander.

Die gestapelte Landschaft ist nicht, wie man vermuten könnte, ein aus der Tradition der durchgängigen zweidimensionalen Landschaftsteppiche abstammender Hybride, sondern etwas ganz anderes: ein Objekt, dessen vertikale Komponente – die scharfe Geschoßkantenlinie – es präzise und entschieden von seiner Umgebung absetzt. Es gehört in die Linie einer bestimmten Strategie der tektonischen Intervention: nicht der totalen Neustrukturierung einer Landschaft, sondern statt dessen ihrer Neuorientierung durch Hineinsetzen eines einzelnen Elements – Eisberg, Monolith, gelandetes Raumschiff –, eines Objekttyps also, dessen Bedeutung in seiner Autonomie und seiner Herauslösung aus dem Umgebenden liegt. Das in einer grünen Parklandschaft freistehende Großobjekt ist auch über den Mainstream der Moderne des 20. Jahrhunderts auf uns gekommen, etwa Le Corbusiers Unité d'Habitation in Marseille oder Mies van der Rohes Haus Farnsworth. Heute hat sich diese Objekt-Feld-Beziehung ihrer utopischen Zielsetzungen entledigt. Der Park ist nicht länger idealisierte Natur, sondern schlicht ein zersiedeltes Gebiet, ein sich selbst fortpflanzender Fleck aus Infrastruktur, Verkehrsnetz, grünen Restflächen und abgegrenzten Zonen für autonome Nutzungen. Das Mega-Vertikal-Objekt fungiert in solchen Kontexten als Landmarke, es ist ein Ausbruch von Masse, der seiner Umgebung Maß und Orientierung verleiht.

1964 publizierte Hans Hollein das emblematische Bild eines Flugzeugträgers auf einem Hügel, der wie eine Akropolis über fruchtbarem Ackerland thront. Ob Schiff oder Stadt – dieses autonome und autarke Objekt bildet einen so extremen Kontrast zu seiner idealisierten landschaftlichen Umgebung, daß der Betrachter keinen Zweifel hegen konnte, darin das Endspiel der modernen utopischen Maschinen-Landschafts-Dialektik zu erleben. Bezeichnenderweise wählte Hollein einen Flugzeugträger für seine Polemik: Das leere Flugdeck bringt von neuem die horizontale Dimension ins Spiel, bildet ein Feld für abhebende Vektoren und Verbindungen zum nichtdefinierten Anderswo.

Kumulative bzw. expansive Eingriffe in die Landschaft finden ihre Parallele nicht nur in den derzeit angewandten digitalen bzw. analogen Entwurfsstrategien, sondern auch in der den meisten Siedlungsmustern zugrundeliegenden Dialektik. Die historische europäische Stadt war in den Grenzen ihrer Befestigungsanlagen gefangen und entwickelte sich also in die Vertikale, in einem sukzessiven Ablagerungsprozeß historischer Schichten. Dagegen funktionierte das von der amerikanischen Landvermessung unter Jefferson definierte Raster als eine Art horizontales konzeptuelles Netz, das von der Ostküste aus gen Westen ausgeworfen wurde, um die riesigen Prärien dem Reich rationaler Kalibrierung einzuverleiben. Natürliche Brüche, Tafelberge, Flüsse sowie Eisenerzvorkommen, welche die Magneten der Landvermesser zu Verwerfungen im Raster verführten, verliehen dieser systematischen Mega-Expansion eine poetische Dimension. Es ist kein Zufall, daß dies eine der wichtigsten Referenzen für Barkow und Leibinger bildet. Ihre Biosphäre Potsdam wurde mit einem feinen Gespür für eine präriegleiche horizontale Expansion modelliert, nicht als axialer Fokus und Verbindungsknoten der europäischen Gartenkunst, sondern mit einer impliziten vektoriellen Projektion in ein nichtdefiniertes Anderswo.

EIN MASS FÜR DIE FELDER DES JUST-IN-TIME

Die heute ganz Europa überziehenden Transportnetze sind dabei, unseren Begriff vom „Hier" als einzigartigem Zustand, als Ort aufzulösen. Die Datenfernübertragung rückt alle Orte zur gleichen Zeit in die gleiche Nähe. Anderswo – diese Zone, welche von Physikern als jenseits des Ereignishorizonts einer Singularität liegend definiert wird, ist jetzt überall. Unsichtbare Kräfte wie die digitalisierte Logistik des Just-in-Time-Liefernetzes prägen unsere zunehmend verstreuten und entwurzelten Siedlungsmuster und -zyklen offenbar stärker als der Charakter und die Faltungen der tatsächlichen Landschaft. Jedes Mal, wenn Architektur und Landschaft auf der grünen Wiese oder im Gewerbepark zusammentreffen, haben sie das Potential und die Aufgabe, ihren Status als primäre Bezugsgröße zu behaupten, die Komplexität der jeweils vorhandenen Situation zu relativieren und ihr ein Maß zu geben. Die Biosphäre Potsdam stellt sich dieser Herausforderung in anregender und aufregender Weise.

Architekturtheoretiker werfen heute viel von der physischen Last ihrer mühseligen Disziplin ab und stürzen sich fieberhaft ins Erfinden einer postdigitalen Architektursyntax. Faltungen, Felder und Teppiche entstehen in Hülle und Fülle, wie auch programmierte Hybride, dichte Netzwerke und Kontinuen des Inneren. Die allem zugrundeliegende Metapher heißt „Landschaft". Im Aggregatzustand schwereloser Diagramme sind derartige Cyber-Architektur-Landschaften endlos formbar; wenn sie die Grenze vom virtuellen zum realen Raum überschreiten wollen, müssen sie nicht nur formale, sondern auch physische und tektonische Grenzen berücksichtigen.

Mit entwaffnender Einfachheit relativiert die Biosphäre die derzeitige hypothetische Felddebatte. Das Dach ist schlicht und selbstverständlich da, eine künstliche Platte, eine erhöhte Scheibe Landschaft komplett mit grünen Streifen. Ihre orthogonale Silhouette und ihr Akzeptieren der tektonischen Logik von 1,5 m tiefen und 35 m langen Fertigbetonträgern unterscheidet sie von den Formverzerrungen ihrer theoretisch erzeugten Gegenspieler. Wir denken dabei an das Deck von Holleins Flugzeugträger, an das über Mies' Neuer Nationalgalerie in Berlin schwebende Dach, an eine Architektur, die intelligent und ökonomisch zwischen der Oberfläche des Erdbodens und tektonischen Überlagerungen unterscheidet.

Die wahre Bedeutung der Biosphäre liegt darin, daß sie uns nicht mit theoretischen Abstraktionen von ihrem Ort distanziert, sondern uns darin erdet, verankert. Diese Ortbildung ist Maß-gebend, nicht nur im Rahmen der unmittelbaren landschaftlichen Umgebung, sondern auch im flüchtigen Reich des Digitalen. Dem Besucher wird ein direktes, intensives Erlebnis angeboten, er wird durch prismatisch geformte Täler und mittels Rampen über geharkte Hügel aus geisterhaft leuchtenden Pixelblüten geführt und auf die Hochebenen des Daches erhoben. Innen wie außen gibt das epische Maß der Landschaft den Maßstab.

Durch diese großartige Szenographie zieht sich ein zweites, tektonisches Maß. Wie hängender Wein oder ein Wald aus systematisch aufgereihten Schößlingen sind die filigranen Fassaden zwischen Dach und Boden gespannt. Angemessen einfache, fast industrielle Oberlichtbänder setzen diese tektonische Sprache über das schwebende Dach fort. Hier ist die augenfällige serielle Struktur von Zäunen oder landwirtschaftlichen Bauten am Werk. Dieses Projekt überwindet den Gegensatz von Natur und Menschenwerk – jenes Relikt der Kristallpaläste des 19. Jahrhunderts –, es überwindet die geodätischen Kuppeln Buckminster Fullers und die hermetische Insularität heutiger Raumschiff-Kokon-Gewächshäuser wie etwa Norman Fosters jüngstem „Glashaus" in den National Botanic Gardens von Wales. Seine subtilen Schichtungen verweben Vertikales und Horizontales. Diese Architektur erfüllt das ehrgeizige Ziel des amerikanischen Land Art-Künstlers Robert Smithson, der von seinem Spiral Jetty sagte: „Letzten Endes lasse ich den Standort bestimmen, was ich baue."

Peter Wilson, Architekt, Büro Bolles-Wilson, Münster

Essay by **Peter Wilson**

The Epic Scale of Landscape Notes on the Potsdam Biosphere

Some ten years ago I sketched a small landscape in my notebook. It was about the time when computers were beginning to replace hand drafting in architectural offices, when images took off on digital trajectories, when text broke loose from the tyranny of the mechanical and started to drift across any available surface. My sketch was not remarkable except that it was done in sunshine on wind-harassed paper. The landscape was not Brandenburg, but could well have been. A dark line of trees connected the left and right sides of the image. Grey paint on the upper page suggested atmospheric turbulence. Some flame-like orange in the tree band implied a particular phase in the yearly growth cycle. To the right a hand-written list ran from top to bottom ....*swivel tilt move persp yes hide no carpet off frame auto y draw plot three iso axo undump view type round advance zoom.....*

This now familiar menu type instructs not only computers, but also our eyes. Our perceptive apparatus, our "ways of seeing", have been reprogrammed. We now accept without a blink of the eye that text can fly, that previously discrete objects can morph into any number of foreign bodies, that the privileged singular viewing point of classical perspective has been replaced by a new form of visual and informational flux. Post-digital perception is about disconnected information bits, visual fragments whose sequences reveal no higher order, where the shock value of discontinuity with which surrealism once challenged convention has now itself become convention. The status of landscape has not remained immune to this radical repositioning. As a metaphor, "landscape" provides a topographic analogy for new data fields. This situation calls for a reciprocal post-digital reconstitution of the possibilities of landscape.

A characteristic relation to landscape is a fundamental attribute of any particular time. The English landscape gardener Humphrey Repton neatly captured Georgian England by stating that "a gentleman let alone a gentlewoman could not be expected to look out of the window, when away from society, on to anything other than beautifully rolling green turf and parkland". One hundred years later, Adolf Loos insisted that "a gentleman does not look out of the window". Lenné's Potsdam Bretzelgardens also characterized the nineteenth century; could a National Horticultural Show in Potsdam do the same for the current moment in history?

How then do we access actual landscape, metric space whose topographic dimension is still measured experientially, bodily? How do we relate this measured space to the topological space of information technology, which co-opts the idea of landscape in indeterminate fields of continuities and relations?

Contemporary field theory prioritizes not the form of the whole but internal relations. A field is a general condition as opposed to the unique characteristics of a specific place. Contemporary field theory also encompasses dynamic spatial relationships: flocking of birds and similar highly complex phenomena can be rendered as a quantifiable spatial matrix – a shift from a static to a fluid paradigm. But what of landscape itself? Should it now also oscillate like waves in response to the complexity of momentary conditions or does it gain a new significance as a background and a register against which hyperactive contemporary trajectories can be measured?

HORIZONTAL VERTICAL

Dutch field theory, i.e. the varying arrangements of diverse but internally consistent landscape parcels, is essentially a two-dimensional game. Holland is a flat country. It is a game of collaged and widely differing densities – the Netherlands is a small country. It is also a game which, like our contemporary media, makes little distinction between the artificial and any idea of the authentic or the natural: the constructed (Polder) landscape of Holland is a man-made artefact. The Dutch EXPO-Pavilion in Hanover by MVRDV neatly side-steps the inherent political and economic difficulties of appropriating excessive terrain by stacking vertically. Five landscapes piled on top of each other are, following the logic of the Big Mac, five times better than a neighbouring single level plot.

The stacked landscape is not, as one might expect, a hybrid deriving from the tradition of continuous two-dimensional landscape tapestries. It is quite a different animal, an object whose vertical component, the cut line of its edges, separates it precisely and categorically from its surroundings. It belongs to a certain strategy for tectonic intervention, not the total re-figuring of a landscape, instead the insertion of a single re-orienting element: the iceberg, the monolith, the landed spaceship – an object type whose significance lies in its autonomy and its dissociation from its surroundings. The large object, free-standing in a green park-like landscape, also comes to us via mainstream twentieth-century modernism, the Unité d'Habitation in Marseille by Le Corbusier or the Farnsworth House by Mies van der Rohe. Today this object-field relationship has shed its utopian aspirations. The park is no longer idealized nature, it is now simply sprawl, a self-perpetuating smudge of infrastructure, transport networks, green leftovers and enclosures for autonomous programmes. The mega-vertical object in such contexts performs the function of landmark: an outbreak of mass giving measure and orientation to its surroundings.

In 1964 Hans Hollein published an emblematic image of a hilltop aircraft-carrier dominating acropolis-like a fertile agricultural landscape. Ship or city, this autonomous, self-contained object stands in such extreme contrast to its idealized context that the viewer was left in no doubt that this was the end game of the modernist utopian machine-landscape dialectic. The choice of an aircraft-carrier in the Hollein polemic is significant, its empty landing deck reintroduces a horizontal dimension, a field for vectoral launchings and connections to unspecified elsewheres.

Cumulative and expansive landscape interventions find their parallel not only in contemporary digital and analogue operative strategies, but also as the fundamental dialectic of most settlement patterns. The historic European city bound by the absolute limit of its defensive battlements evolved vertically, a sedimenting of historic layer on historic layer. The Jefferson survey grid in America on the other hand functioned as a sort of horizontal conceptual net thrown out from the East Coast to bring the vast prairie hinterland into the realm of rational calibration. Natural disruptions, mesas, rivers and iron ore deposits which seduced surveyors' magnets into warping the grid give a poetic dimension to this system of mega-extension. It is no coincidence that this is one of the favourite references of Barkow and Leibinger. Their Potsdam Biosphere is sculpted with a feeling for prairie-like horizontal extension, not the axial focusing and connection of European gardens but an implied vectorial projection to unspecified elsewheres.

GIVING MEASURE TO JUST-IN-TIME FIELDS

Today ubiquitous transport networks covering the entire European landscape are eroding our awareness of here as a unique condition, as a place. Teletransported information is simultaneously rendering all places equally near. Elsewhere, that zone defined by physicists as beyond the event horizon of a singularity, is now everywhere. Invisible forces like the digitized logistics of Just-in-Time delivery networks seem to condition our increasingly dispersed and displaced habitation patterns and cycles more than the character and folds of the actual landscape. Each time architecture and landscape coincide in green field or business park they have the potential and the responsibility to assert their status as a primary referent, to relativize the complexity of momentary conditions, to give measure. The Potsdam Biosphere provocatively and evocatively meets this challenge.

Abandoning much of the physical baggage of their cumbersome discipline, architectural academicians are today feverishly engaged in inventing a post-digital architectural syntax. Folds, fields and carpets abound, along with programmed hybridity, dense networks, continuous interiority. Landscape is the underlying metaphor. Infinitely malleable at the stage of gravityless diagrams, such cyber-generated architectural landscapes must, if they are to cross the virtual-real border, take into account not only formal but also physical and tectonic limitations.

The Potsdam Biosphere relativizes the current hypothetical field debate by its disarming simplicity. The roof is simply and confidently there, an artificial plate, an elevated slice of landscape complete with green stripes. Its rectangular silhouette and its acceptance of the tectonic logic of precast concrete beams 1.5 metre deep and 35 meter wide distinguish it from the formal distortions of theoretically generated counterparts. We think here of the deck of Hollein's aircraft-carrier, of the hovering roof of Mies's New National Gallery in Berlin, of an architecture which intelligently and economically distinguishes between the surface of the earth and further tectonic overlays.

The real significance of the Biosphere is that it does not distance us from its site with theoretical abstractions, instead it grounds, it anchors. This place-making gives measure not only within the immediate landscape, but also in the ethereal realm of the digital. The visitor is offered direct and intense experience, led through prismatic valleys, ramped over raked mounds of lurid pixel flowers, elevated to the high planes of the roof. From inside and from outside the scale is the epic scale of landscape.

Woven through this grand scenography is a tectonic second scale. Like hanging vines or a forest of systematized saplings the filigree façades are stretched between roof and ground. Appropriately simple, almost industrial roof-light strips repeat this tectonic language horizontally across the hovering roof slab. The obvious repetitive logic of fences or agricultural buildings is at work here.

This project transcends the oppositional nature-artifice dialectic, a relic of nineteenth-century glass palaces, Buckminster Fuller domes and the hermetic insularity of contemporary circular spaceship cocoon greenhouses like Norman Foster's recent Glasshouse in the National Botanical Gardens of Wales. Its subtle layering intermeshes vertical and horizontal. It is an architecture that fulfils the ambition of the American land artist Robert Smithson who said of his Spiral Jetty: "In the end I would let the site determine what I would build."

Peter Wilson, architect, Büro Bolles-Wilson, Münster, Germany

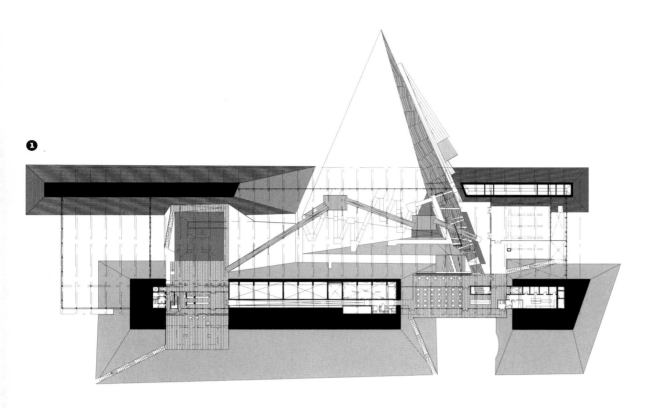

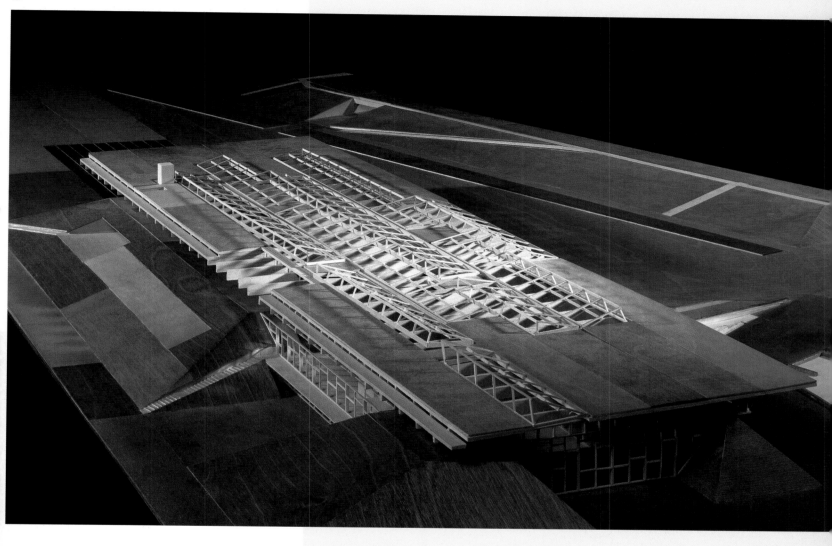

❶ Grundriß des Entwurfs von Barkow Leibinger, Berlin.

Floor plan of the design by Barkow Leibinger, Berlin.

❷ Die Biosphäre verbindet das bau- und gartenhistorische Erbe Potsdams mit dem Zeitgeist der Gegenwart.

The Biosphere links Potsdam's architectural and garden-historical heritage with the spirit of the present.

❸ Im Arbeitsmodell wird die Integration von Bauwerk und Landschaft deutlich.

The working model shows clearly how the building and the landscape are integrated.

❸

❶ Peter Wilson vergleicht die starke
Präsenz der Biosphäre mit dem
Image der Holleinschen „Flug-
zeugträgerstadt" von 1964.

Peter Wilson compares the powerful presence of the Biosphere with
the image of Hollein's 1964
"Aircraft-carrier town".

❷ Außen wie innen kehrt das Motiv
der Wälle wieder und eröffnet
Perspektiven aus verschiedenen
Höhen.

The rampart motif recurs outside
and inside and opens up perspec-
tives from different heights.

❸ Der Platz vor der Biosphäre schiebt
sich als Platte in den Park hinein.

The square in front of the Biosphere
forms a plateau that thrusts into
the park.

1

❶ Während der Bundesgartenschau werden in der Halle die Blumen-schauen präsentiert. Ab 2002 wird die Biosphäre dauerhaft als Edu-tainment-Center genutzt.

The flower shows will be presented in the hall during the Bundesgar-tenschau. The Biosphere will be used permanently as an Edutain-ment Centre from 2002.

❷ Nach Süden wirkt das Gebäude ver-schlossen. Die Eingänge liegen in tiefen Einschnitten.

The building seems closed on the south side. The entrances are placed in deep incisions

❸ Auch aus der Luft erinnert das Gebäude an einen gestrandeten Flugzeugträger.

From the air the hall is reminiscent of a stranded aircraft-carrier.

Kunstlandschaft: Entwürfe für die Bornstedter Feldflur

Art(ificial) landscape: designs for the Bornstedt Meadowland

Kai Vöckler

Kunstlandschaft: Entwürfe für die Bornstedter Feldflur

Landschaft wird nicht per se vorgefunden. Sondern Landschaft ist ein bestimmter Ausschnitt, ein Teil der Natur, der sich in Landschaft verwandelt, wenn er sich der ästhetischen Erfahrung erschließt. Landschaft ist das Produkt einer Wahrnehmungsleistung. Die Voraussetzung, Natur als ästhetisches Phänomen zu betrachten, ist erst seit der fortschreitenden Naturbeherrschung und Urbanisierung gegeben. Mit der Naturausbeutung geht die Entwicklung des ästhetischen Naturerlebnisses einher.

In den vergangenen Jahrhunderten war es Aufgabe der Künste, die Wahrnehmung von Landschaften zu trainieren – auch dieser Blick wollte gelernt sein. Heute sind es die massenmedial und werbestrategisch inszenierten Landschaftsbilder, die als Wahrnehmungsreize den Alltag bestimmen; als verinnerlichte Vorstellungsbilder prägen sie die Landschaftserfahrung. Diesen medial vorgeprägten Blickweisen hat sich die Realität zu beugen, denn das Erleben von Landschaft vor Ort findet innerhalb vorgefertigter Erwartungsmuster statt. Reiseprospekte präformieren diesen Blick, nehmen die Bilder vorweg, denen sich die touristischen Orte gestalterisch anzupassen haben. Was nicht ins Bild paßt, wird am Ausflugziel durch den richtigen fotografischen Ausschnitt visuell beseitigt.

So steht es auch um die Kulturlandschaft. Daß das Land nicht nur Naturraum, sondern auch Wirtschaftsraum ist, ist jedem Bauern selbstverständlich. Erst aus der Perspektive des Städters erhält das Land eine Funktion als Erholungsraum. Unsere Vorstellung von Kulturlandschaft orientiert sich dabei an einem vorindustriellen Zustand, wie er uns beispielsweise aus den Bildern der niederländischen Landschaftsmalerei des 17. Jahrhunderts vertraut ist. Das idealisierte Bild einer präindustriellen, bäuerlich geprägten Landschaft drückt die Sehnsucht nach einem Zustand aus, in dem sich menschliche Kultur und Natur scheinbar im Einklang befinden. Tatsächlich beschreibt das vorindustrielle Bild aber nur den seinerzeit fortschrittlichsten Stand der Naturausbeutung. Spätestens seit der Einführung von Liebigs Kunstdünger in die Landwirtschaft sind künstliche und natürliche Prozesse auf eine Weise miteinander verbunden, die einer Erfahrung, die sich an bildhaften Naturvorstellungen orientiert, unzugänglich bleiben. Zudem hat die Intensivierung der landwirtschaftlichen Produktion, einhergehend mit der Mechanisierung und Rationalisierung landwirtschaftlicher Betriebe, ebenso wie die fortschreitende Verstädterung mit ihrer Streuung von Siedlungsflächen das Landschaftsgefüge soweit überformt, daß es uns schwerfällt, dieses mit den tradierten Vorstellungen einer Natur- oder Kulturlandschaft in Einklang zu bringen.

Ein Beispiel dafür ist die Bornstedter Feldflur, einer der vier räumlichen Schwerpunkte der Bundesgartenschau. Im Norden Potsdams gelegen, bildet sie den Übergang vom Stadtgebiet in den Landschaftsraum der Bornimer Feldflur. Gekennzeichnet ist dieser ca. 65 ha große Übergangsraum durch die heterogene Mischung aus Kleingärten, Gewerbebetrieben, Brachflächen, Acker und Wald, wie sie typisch ist für eine randstädtische Lage.

Eine besondere Bedeutung kommt der Feldflur als Teil der von Peter Joseph Lenné im 19. Jahrhundert gestalteten Kulturlandschaft zu. Seine Vorstellung der „Landesverschönerung", die Potsdam mit der umgebenden Landschaft durch ein differenziertes System von Blickbezügen verband, bezog nicht nur die architektonischen und landschaftlichen Besonderheiten ein, sondern auch die agrarisch genutzten Flächen. Die Strukturierung der Bornimer Feldflur mit Wegen, Alleen, Hecken und Remisen durch Lenné veränderte sich mit der landwirtschaftlichen Produktion und fortschreitenden Zersiedelung. Zur BUGA 2001 wurde durch das Amt für Flurneuordnung und ländliche Entwicklung die kritische Rekonstruktion der Lennéschen Feldflur betrieben. Darauf aufbauend lobte der Entwicklungsträger Bornstedter Feld den Wettbewerb „Bornstedter Feldflur" aus. Er stellte nicht die Rekonstruktion, sondern die Interpretation dieses Gebietes mit Mitteln zeitgenössischer Kunst und Gartenarchitektur zur Aufgabe – und formulierte damit eine besondere Herausforderung für die Teilnehmer. Die nach einem Bewerbungsverfahren ausgewählten 15 Arbeitsgemeinschaften aus Künstlern, Landschaftsarchitekten und Agraringenieuren standen vor der Aufgabe, eine zeitgemäße Interpretation einer Kulturlandschaft unter Einbeziehung aktueller Themen der Landwirtschaft zu entwickeln und zugleich die Bedingungen zu reflektieren, unter denen in einer modernen, technisierten Umwelt Landschaft wahrgenommen wird. Landschaftsarchitekten, Künstler und Agraringenieure waren aufgefordert, gemeinsam ein integratives Gesamtkonzept für eine weitgehend temporäre Gestaltung der Feldflur während der Bundesgartenschau zu entwickeln. Aufgabenstellung und Verfahren haben zu sehr unterschiedlichen, aber hochinteressanten Ergebnissen geführt.

Das Zürcher Landschaftsarchitekturbüro Rotzler Krebs Partner entwickelte mit dem Berliner Künstler Otmar Sattel und dem Agraringenieur Hermann Giebelhausen ein Konzept, welches das Lennésche Motto, das Nützliche sei mit dem Schönen zu verknüpfen, wortwörtlich nimmt und die Schönheit des Nützlichen herausarbeitet. Der mit dem 1. Preis bedachte Entwurf konzipiert die Feldflur als Weidelandschaft und hinterfragt auf subtile Weise unsere Vorstellungen einer Nutztierhaltung. Einerseits sollen die Besucher Rinder, Pferde, Schafe, Schweine oder Ziegen in ihrer gewöhnlichen Lebensart bestaunen dürfen, andererseits wird eine sentimentale Sicht auf deren Lebensbedingungen durch den Einsatz zahlreicher verfremdender Gestaltungsmittel verhindert: Stahlcontainer dienen als Unterstände, oder es wird in ihnen das landwirtschaftliche Produkt Milch angeboten; auch kann auf Monitoren einer anderen Landschaftswahrnehmung gefolgt werden – derjenigen einer Kuh, deren Blick auf Weidelgras, Rotschwingel, Knaulgras, Weißklee mittels am Kopf befestigter Minivideokameras übertragen wird. Und es werden eher unanschauliche Bioprozesse wie Vergärung und Verrottung wahrnehmbar gemacht.

Dagegen übersetzt der 2. Preisträger, das holländische Landschaftsarchitekturbüro West 8 in Zusammenarbeit mit der Berliner Künstlerin Inge Mahn, den in großen Feldschlägen stattfindenden Anbau von Kulturpflanzen in ein kleinräumiges Mosaik aus Feldern, die zu verschiedenen Jahreszeiten blühen und geerntet werden. Die Strukturierung der Felder durch Strohhecken gibt ebenso wie die Errichtung temporärer Strohskulpturen dem Entwurf einen volkstümlichen Charakter, der aber kaum Anstoß zur Auseinandersetzung mit der Realität der Landwirtschaft geben dürfte.

Das mit dem 3. Preis bedachte Konzept der Arbeitsgemeinschaft des Landschaftsarchitekturbüros ST raum a. und der Künstlerin Francis Zeischegg, beide aus Berlin, differenziert die Feldflur in eine von landwirtschaftlicher Nutzung geprägte Feldlandschaft und eine haus- und hofnahe, kleinflächige Hoflandschaft, um auf diese Weise den Übergang vom Siedlungsbereich in den Landschaftsraum zu akzentuieren. Unterstützt wird dieser Ansatz durch streifenartige, mit Sonderkulturen bepflanzte Bänder, die sich in die benachbarte Bornimer Feldflur ziehen. Der Entwurf, der eine differenzierte Gestaltung der farbästhetischen wie auch landschaftsarchitektonischen Aspekte groß- und kleinflächiger Nutzungsformen aufweist, setzt auf eine klare und geometrische Formensprache, um das heterogene Wettbewerbsgebiet gestalterisch zu ordnen. Unterstützt wird dieses Unterfangen durch sieben im Entwurfsgebiet verteilte Raummodule, die durch Sehschlitze, Gucklöcher, Dachöff-

nungen und Transparenzkabinen unterschiedliche Blickweisen auf die Landschaft formieren. Das Blickachsenmotiv der Lennéschen Landschaftskonzeption wird aufgegriffen und neu interpretiert: So geraten neben Pfingst- und Ruinenberg auch eine Mülldeponie oder eine Agrargenossenschaft in den Blick.

Das komplexe Blickachsensystem Lennés dekonstruieren die Berliner Landschaftsarchitekten Annette und Daniel Sprenger gemeinsam mit dem Potsdamer Künstler Jörg Schlinke. Der ganz auf die künstlerische Intervention setzende Entwurf sieht den Abwurf von 90 über zwei Meter großen Betonpfeilern in die Feldflur vor. Einem ordnenden Zugriff auf das Wettbewerbsgebiet wurde entsagt und statt dessen die Feldflur in all ihrer Widersprüchlichkeit durch eine radikale künstlerische Setzung thematisiert. Der Verkauf von in Pfeilform gewachsenen Gurken als eßbares Kunstobjekt schafft zudem eine angenehme ironische Distanz zum eigenen Vorhaben.

Auch der Landschaftsarchitekt Christoph Geskes und die Künstlerin Simone Mangos aus Berlin wollen die Feldflur nicht mehr ordnen. In die landwirtschaftlichen Flächen werden verschieden bestellte, kleinflächige Felder eingefügt, die sich wie Inseln in eine diffus strukturierte Umgebung einbetten. Entsprechend sollen mittels Stahlskulpturen, die als Reflektorplatten dienen, akustische Brennpunkte entstehen, die umgebende Geräusche verdichten.

Der Berliner Landschaftsarchitektin Ariane Röntz und dem amerikanischen Künstler Edward A. Dormer gelang der Entwurf eines farbenprächtigen, als „13-Felder-Wirtschaft" konzipierten Bandes, das sich in die Bornimer Feldflur zieht und eine kraftvolle räumliche Intervention darstellt.

Die Bornstedter Feldflur wird in allen diesen Gestaltungsvorschlägen wesentlich als eine Landschaft des Übergangs begriffen. Die Durchmischung städtischer und ländlicher Strukturen ebenso wie die veränderten Bedingungen landwirtschaftlicher Produktion haben hier einen neuen, entstrukturierten Raum hervorgebracht, der mit der traditionellen Vorstellung von einer Kulturlandschaft nicht mehr in Einklang zu bringen ist.

Für alle Entwürfe ist kennzeichnend, daß sie im Spannungsfeld von Künstlichem und Virtuellem einerseits und Natürlichem andererseits eine zeitgemäße Interpretation von Landschaft und den Bedingungen, unter denen wir sie wahrnehmen, entwickeln. Auch wenn es uns schwerfällt, die im Zuge der modernen Zivilisation entstandenen Veränderungen unserer Umwelt als Landschaft zu begreifen, so sind hier doch Perspektiven für eine neue Sichtweise entworfen worden.

Kai Vöckler ist Künstler und Kurator.

Kai Vöckler

Art(ificial) landscape: designs for the Bornstedt Meadowland

Landscape is not just simply there. Landscape is a certain part of nature, a part that is transformed into landscape when it is opened up to aesthetic experience. Landscape is the product of an effort of perception. But the idea that nature should be considered as an aesthetic phenomenon has existed only since man imposed progressive urbanization and domination over nature. The development of the aesthetic experience of nature goes hand in hand with the exploitation of nature.

In previous centuries it was the role of the arts to train people how to look at landscapes – this was something that had to be learned as well. Today it is landscape as presented by the mass media and advertising strategists that determines the way we perceive everyday life; a set of internalized imaginative constructs shaping our experience of landscape. Reality has to submit to these media-predetermined ways of looking at things: experiencing landscape on the spot takes place within prefabricated expectation patterns. Travel brochures pre-shape this view by anticipating the images that tourist spots have to conform to. Anything that does not fit in with the image will be set on one side visually at the destination by choosing the correct photographic detail.

The same thing applies to landscape as cultivated and developed by man. Every farmer knows that the countryside is not just a natural space, but also a commercial space. It is only from the point of view of the city-dweller that such land is deemed to be enjoyed as a recreational facility. Here our idea of landscape relates to a pre-industrial condition, with which we are familiar from 17th century Dutch landscape painting, for example. This idealized image of a pre-industrial landscape shaped by farming expresses our longing for a condition in which human culture and nature seem to be in harmony. But in fact the pre-industrial image describes only the most advanced state of exploitation of nature at the time. Since the introduction of Liebig's artificial fertilizer into agriculture at the latest, artificial and natural processes have been linked in a way that is impenetrable to an experience guided by visual ideas of nature. At the same time agricultural production was intensified, going hand in hand with the mechanization and rationalization of agricultural processes. This and progressive urbanization, with its dispersal of settlements, so transformed the structure of the landscape that it is difficult for us to reconcile this with traditional ideas of a natural or cultivated landscape.

One example of this is the Bornstedter Feldflur (Bornstedt Meadowland), which is one of the Show's four spatial focuses. It is set in the north of Potsdam, and forms a transition from the town to the landscape of the Bornimer Feldflur. The transition space occupies about 65 hectares and is characterized by a heterogeneous mixture of allotments, light industry, waste land, farmland and woods, all typical of an area on the edge of a town.

The Meadowland is of particular importance as it forms part of the landscape that Peter Joseph Lenné designed and cultivated in the 19th century. His idea of "beautified land" linking Potsdam with the surrounding countryside by means of a sophisticated system of related views did not just include just special architectural and landscape features, but also the areas that were used for agriculture. The structure of the Bornim Meadowland with it paths, avenues, hedges and thickets goes back to Lenné. But it changed with agricultural production methods and severe overdevelopment. The critical reconstruction of Lenné's Meadowland was carried out by the office of land reallocation and rural development for the National Horticultural Show 2001. The developer Entwicklungsträger Bornstedter Feld announced the "Bornstedter Feldflur" competition on this basis.

The competition posed a particularly difficult challenge for entrants. After applications had been submitted, 15 working groups made up of artists, landscape architects and agricultural engineers were faced with the task of developing an up-to-date interpretation of a man-made landscape, including current agricultural aspects, and at the same time reflecting on the conditions under which landscape is perceived in a modern world dominated by technology. Landscape architects, artists and agricultural engineers were asked to work together to develop an integrated overall concept for a largely temporary design for the Meadowland during the National Horticultural Show. The brief and the process led to very different but extremely interesting results.

The Zurich landscape architects Rotzler Krebs Partner, working with the Berlin artist Otmar Sattel and agricultural engineer Hermann Giebelhausen, developed a concept that takes Lenné's motto of combining the useful with the beautiful literally: it draws out the beauty of what is useful. The design that won 1st prize saw the meadowland as a grazing landscape, and subtly questions our ideas about keeping animals for our use. The intention is that visitors should be able to admire cattle, horses, sheep, pigs or goats in their normal habitat, but any risk of sentimentality is removed by using a number of alienating design devices: steel containers are used as shelters, or to offer milk for sale as an agricultural product; or a different perception of the countryside can be seen on monitors – a cow's eye view of Lolium perennae, red fescue, cocksfoot and white clover is transmitted via mini video cameras attached to their heads. And essentially hidden biological processes like fermentation and rotting are made visible.

In contrast with this, the winners of the 2nd prize, the Dutch landscape architects West 8 working with the Berlin artist Inge Mahn, translated the kind of planting that is usual in large cultivated areas into a small and intricate mosaic of fields that blossom and are harvested at different times of the year. The fields are divided up by straw hedges, and this and temporary straw sculptures give the design a popular character which, however, would be unlikely to stimulate people to address the realities of agriculture.

The winners of the 3rd prize, landscape architects ST raum a. and the artist Francis Zeischegg, both from Berlin, came up with the idea of breaking the meadowland down into a field landscape shaped by agricultural use and a small farm landscape of the type that emerges close to house and yard, as a way of accentuating the transition from settlement to the open landscape. This approach is reinforced by bands planted with special crops running into the adjacent Bornim Meadowland. This design, which comes up with a differentiated approach to colour-aesthetic and landscape-agricultural aspects of large- and small-scale ways of using land, relies on a clear and geometrical formal language to impose order on the heterogeneous competition area. This venture is supported by seven modules distributed around the area whose viewing slits, peepholes, roof apertures and transparent cabins provide different ways of looking at the landscape. The viewing axes that underpinned Lenné's concept of landscape are taken up and re-interpreted: in this way the Pfingstberg and the Ruinenberg become part of the view, and so do a refuse dump or an agricultural cooperative.

The Berlin landscape architects Annette and Daniel Sprenger working with the Potsdam artist Jörg Schlinke deconstruct Lenné's complex system of visual axes. This design relies entirely on artistic intervention and proposes dropping 90 concrete arrows over two metres long into the meadowland. Any attempt to impose order on the competition area was rejected and instead of this the full contradictory nature of the site was addressed by a radical artistic proposition. The proposed sale of cucumbers grown in the

shape of arrows suggests that the artists have a pleasant sense of ironic distance from their own project.

Landscape architect Christoph Geskes and artist Simone Mangos of Berlin do not want to impose order on the meadowland either. Differently cultivated small fields are fitted into the agricultural areas, bedding into diffusely structured surroundings like islands. Corresponding acoustic focal points, condensing the sounds from the immediate vicinity, are created by means of steel sculptures serving as reflector plates.

The Berlin landscape architect Ariane Röntz and the American artist Edward A. Dormer developed a design for a magnificently colourful band conceived as a "13 field operation": it moves into the Bornim Meadowland and thus represents a powerful spatial intervention.

Essentially, all these design suggestions see the site as a transitional landscape. The mixture of urban and rural structures and the changed conditions of agricultural production have produced a new and destructured space here that no longer fits in with the traditional idea of a landscape as cultivated and developed by man. All the designs share the characteristic of working in the field of tension between the artificial and the virtual on the one hand and the natural on the other to create an up-to-date interpretation of landscape and the conditions under which we perceive it. Even if we still find it difficult to perceive as landscape the changes that have taken place in our surroundings in the course of modern civilization, at least some approaches to a new way of looking at things have been developed here.

Kai Vöckler is an artist and exhibition curator.

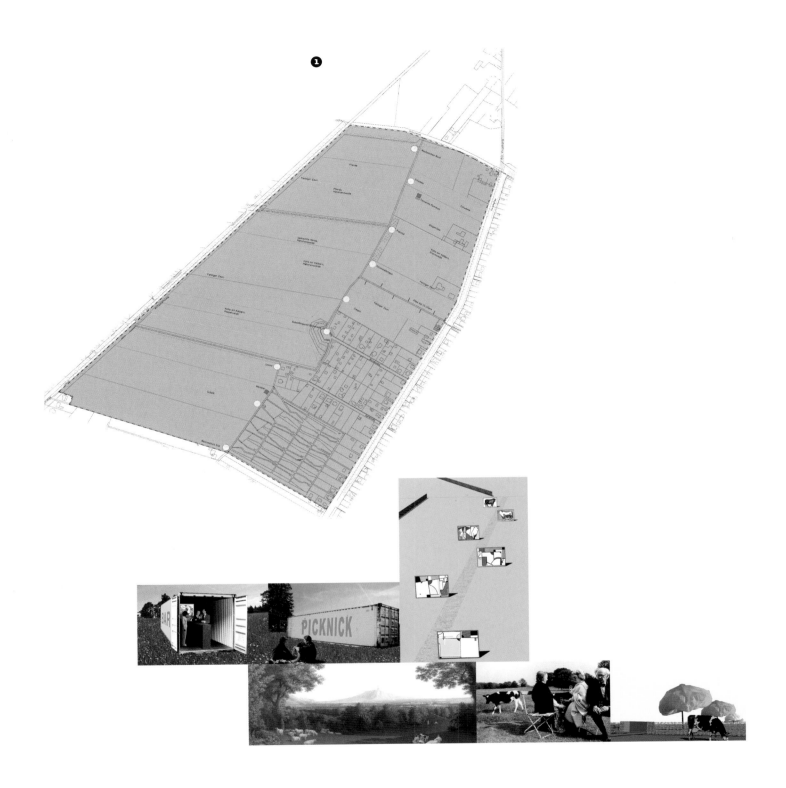

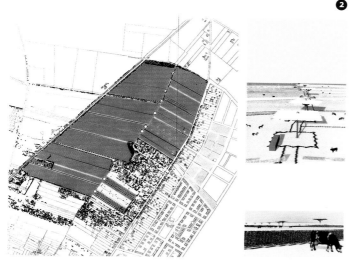

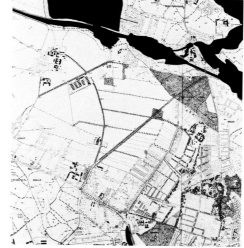

❶ Der 1. Preis blieb letztlich Entwurf. Rotzler Krebs Partner (Zürich), Otmar Sattel (Berlin) und Hermann Giebelhausen (Berlin) lehren den neuen Blick auf die Kulturlandschaft. Prozesse der Stoffumwandlung werden sichtbar. Durch die Kuh hindurch wird der Betrachter Subjekt und Objekt. Denn Kühe mit Videohörnern werden zu VJ's, zu Bildgebern der Gegenwart.

The first prize ultimately never got beyond the drawing board. Rotzler Krebs Partner (Zurich), Otmar Sattel (Berlin) and Hermann Giebelhausen (Berlin) teach us to look at the man-made landscape in a new way. The cow makes the viewer into subject and object: cows with video horns become VJs, the image-providers of the present.

❷ Eine Weidelandschaft macht das Nutztier wieder im Raum sichtbar. Herden von Rindern, Schafen, Ziegen beleben die Feldflur.

A pasture landscape makes domestic animals visible again. Herds of cattle, sheep and goats structure the farmland.

❸ „Lenné mit einem Augenzwinkern" nennen die Entwurfsverfasser ihren Versuch, Kuh, Kult und Kulturlandschaft neu zu inszenieren.

"Lenné with a wink" is the designers' name for their attempt to re-stage cow, cult and cultural landcape.

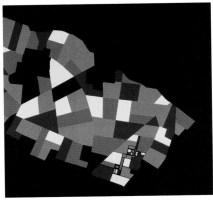

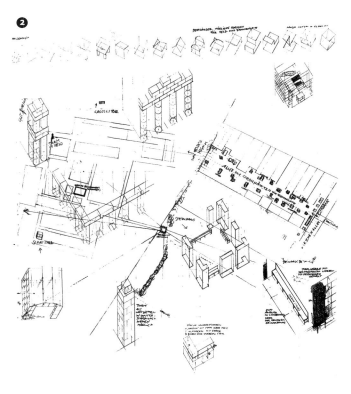

❶

❶ 2. Preis: Die gesamte Bornstedter und Bornimer Feldflur wird im Entwurf von West 8 (Rotterdam), Inge Mahn (Berlin) und Wilfried Hübner (Berlin) zu einem Landschaftsmosaik. Nutzpflanzen in variierender Farbe und Textur verändern das Bild der Landschaft im Wechsel der Jahreszeiten.

2nd prize: the design by West 8 (Rotterdam), Inge Mahn (Berlin) und Wilfried Hübner (Berlin) turns the whole of the Bornstedt and Bornim Meadowland into a landscape mosaic. Economically useful plants in varying colours and textures change the image of the landscape as the seasons pass.

❷ Skulpturen aus Stroh geben der bisherigen Landwirtschaftsfläche einen neuen, prägenden Ausdruck. Vorbilder der Strohbauten sind bekannte Gebäude und Elemente der Potsdamer Kulturlandschaft. Ironie für eine Saison.

Straw sculptures make the former landscape look new in a very striking way. The straw structures are based on familiar buildings and elements of Potsdam's man-made landscape. Irony for one season.

❸

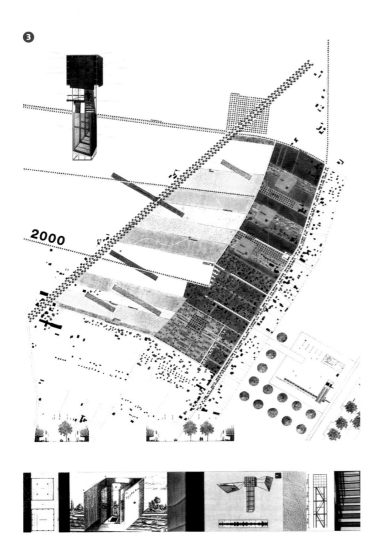

2000

❹

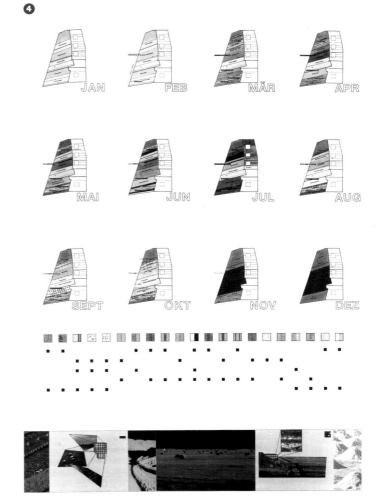

JAN　FEB　MÄR　APR

MAI　JUN　JUL　AUG

SEPT　OKT　NOV　DEZ

❸ 3. Preis: ST raum a., Francis Zeischegg und Anette Wackerhagen (alle Berlin) unterscheiden Hof- und Feldlandschaft. Die Bebauung entlang der Kirschallee wird zur intensiv bewirtschafteten Hoflandschaft, die in die Weite der Feldlandschaft überleitet. In Bändern gepflanzte alte Kultursorten verbinden die Feldfluren. Speziell entwickelte Hochstände bieten den Überblick.

3rd prize: ST raum a., Francis Zeischegg and Anette Wackerhagen (all Berlin) make a distinction between farmland and fields. The development along Kirschallee becomes an intensively managed farm landscape, leading into the open spaces of the fields. The meadows are linked by old cultivated plants arranged in bands. Specially developed stands ensure a good view.

❹ Besonderen Wert legen die Landschaftsarchitekten, die Künstlerin und die Agraringenieurin auf die Inszenierung des Blühkalenders über das Jahr hinweg. Reizvoll ist der ständige Wechsel der Bilder.

The landscape architects, the artist and the agrarian engineer are particularly concerned to make sure that something is in flower throughout the year. The constantly changing images are enchanting.

❶

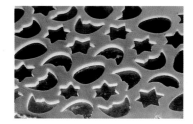

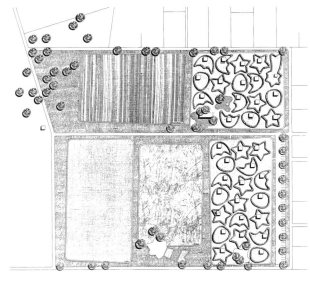

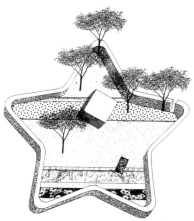

❶ 2. Sonderpreis: Christoph Geskes und Simone Mangos (beide Berlin) widmen sich der Aufgabe spielerischer. Auch sie verzichten auf eine übergeordnete Strukturierung. Stattdessen werden – Plätzchenformen gleichend – kleine Garteninseln in die Feldflur eingestreut.

2ⁿᵈ special prize: Christoph Geskes and Simone Mangos (both Berlin) address the task more playfully. They too choose to do without an ordered structure. Instead little island gardens are strewn around the meadowland – like little biscuit baking tins.

❸

❷

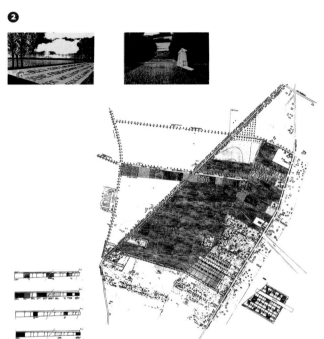

❷ 1. Sonderpreis: Ariane Röntz und Edward A. Dormer gliedern die Feldflur durch die „13-Felder-Wirtschaft"

3ʳᵈ special prize: Ariane Röntz and Edward A. Dormer structure the meadowland by a "13 field operation".

❸ 1. Sonderpreis: Sprenger Landschaftsarchitekten und Jörg Schlinke von der Potsdamer Künstlergruppe BergWerk wagen die radikale Intervention. Neunzig Betonpfeile, jeder über zwei Meter lang, über der Feldflur abgeworfen, stellen die seit Lenné propagierte Ordnung des Raumes radikal in Frage. Die Zufälle des freien Falls der Pfeile weisen den Blick auf Ziele, die unabhängig von den Elementen der Kulturlandschaft auch ins Leere gehen können. Die Erinnerung an die militärische Tradition der Stadt kontrastiert die Harmonie der Potsdamer Landschaft.

1ˢᵗ special prize: Sprenger Landschaftsarchitekten and Jörg Schlinke of the Potsdam group of artists BergWerk risk a radical intervention. Ninety concrete arrows, each over two metres long, dropped over the meadowland, ask radical questions about the way in which Lenné imposed order upon the space. The random fall of the arrows means that they can direct the eye to particular items – or, independent of the cultural landscape, at nothing at all. Memories of the town's military tradition contrast with the harmony of Potsdam's landscape.

Historische Innenstadt und Orte am Fluß
Historic City Centre and Riverside

Historische Innenstadt und Orte am Fluß

Wer in Potsdam den Bahnhof verlassen hat und sich der Innenstadt zuwendet, wird von den Relikten der historischen Silhouette empfangen: Die Kuppel der Nikolaikirche, der Turm des Alten Rathauses und das langgestreckte Dach des Marstalls erheben sich eindrucksvoll über der Havel. Das Entree in die Landeshauptstadt zeigt sich mit kräftigen Fassadenanstrichen und dem satten Grün der Ufer. Ein Sommertag läßt sofort begreifen, welche geradezu paradiesische Enklave Potsdam in der kargen „Streusandbüchse" Brandenburg bildet.

„Historische Innenstadt" und „Orte am Fluß" – schon die Titel dieser zwei Kulissen der Bundesgartenschau bezeichnen ihre örtliche Lage. Noch vor wenigen Jahren vermittelten hier sowohl die Spuren des Zweiten Weltkrieges als auch die baulichen Folgen mangelnden historischen Bewußtseins den Eindruck einer innerstädtischen Peripherie. Heute steht der Besucher in der „grünen Mitte" Potsdams. Die städtischen Projekte der BUGA Potsdam 2001 würdigen das Erbe der letzten Jahrhunderte und kultivieren die Lage am Wasser. Die einst identitätsstiftenden, jedoch zu Beginn der neunziger Jahre desolaten oder gänzlich verschwundenen städtischen Freiräume erforderten jeweils spezifische Entwurfsstrategien, die sowohl den heutigen Anforderungen entsprechen als auch der Gegenwart der originären königlichen Gärten standhalten.

Mit Lustgarten und Altem Markt, der Freundschaftsinsel, dem Nuthepark und dem Platz der Einheit stehen ausgewählte Haltungen aus einem Spektrum von Rekonstruktion bis Neuinterpretation im Maßstab 1:1 zur Diskussion. Ergänzt werden diese zentralen Freiräume Potsdams durch den Ausbau der Promenade Hegelallee, die mit den Plätzen am Nauener Tor und am Jägertor den Verlauf der alten Stadtmauer markiert. Ein Teil des 1961 zugeschütteten Stadtkanals wird freigelegt. Ferner werden ausgewählte Höfe in der barocken Innenstadt neu gestaltet. Darüber hinaus setzt die BUGA Potsdam 2001 Eckpunkte für langfristige Projekte wie die Neugestaltung des Bassinplatzes.

Das Wasser, das in Fluß, Kanal und kleinen Seen die „Insel Potsdam" in den vergangenen Jahrhunderten prägte, wird durch die an der Havel konzentrierten Innenstadtprojekte der Bundesgartenschau Potsdam 2001 wieder stärker

ins Bewußtsein gerückt. Die Ausdehnung des Stadtgebiets nach Süden hat den Schwerpunkt Potsdams geographisch ohnehin wieder in das vergangene Zentrum zurückgeholt. Mit der Entscheidung, statt der Wiedererrichtung der Uferbebauung entlang der Alten Fahrt eine Promenade anzulegen, ergänzen sich die einzelnen Bereiche zur „grünen Mitte", die sowohl nach Norden zu den offenen Baustrukturen der fünfziger und sechziger Jahre vermittelt als auch nach Süden den Ende der neunziger Jahre errichteten Baukomplex um den Hauptbahnhof, das Potsdam-Center, in ein maßstäbliches Verhältnis zur Innenstadt zu setzen versucht.

Lustgarten/Alter Markt

Der Weg in die Stadt über die Lange Brücke verlief in barocker Perspektive schräg auf das Stadtschloß zu und wurde durch dessen Ostfassade auf der einen und die Uferbebauung zum Alten Markt auf der anderen Seite vor die Nikolaikirche geführt. Zwischen Brücke und Schloß, abgegrenzt durch Kolonnaden, begann der Lustgarten, die älteste feudale Grünanlage Potsdams.

Die Aufgabe für den 1997 ausgelobten Wettbewerb „Lustgarten/Alter Markt" war in der Zielsetzung einfach: die Wiedergewinnung des historischen Raums. Denn die Leerräume, die Stadtschloß und Platzrandbebauung hinterlassen haben, führten zum Verlust der Spannung zwischen den beiden Stadtstrukturen, die hier aufeinandertreffen. Die Nikolaikirche, mehr als point de vue für den Landschaftsraum denn für den unmittelbaren Stadtraum konzipiert, stand dadurch unangemessen im Vordergrund.

Die Vorgaben zum Wettbewerb hatten es freilich in sich: Im Bereich des Alten Marktes erlaubten die Beibehaltung der Straßenbahn- und Verkehrstrasse sowie eine schwelende Debatte über Nutzung und Gestalt des Schloßstandortes nur eine temporäre Bespielung. Auf der Fläche des ehemaligen Lustgartens waren die Zuwegung zum Hotel Mercure, einem Hochhausbau aus den sechziger Jahren, und die parallel zur Bahnlinie geplante innerstädtische Entlastungsstraße unumstößliche Parameter.

Das einstimmige Votum der Jury, der Arbeitsgemeinschaft aus Büro freiRaum. Planungsgruppe Stadt Garten Landschaft und Dietz Joppien Architekten den ersten Preis zu geben, würdigte die Überzeugungskraft eines Entwurfs, der in dem sensiblen Bereich den gordischen Knoten löste, nicht zerschlug. „Die Arbeit zeichnet sich dadurch aus, daß mit klaren Strukturen die historischen Raumfolgen aufgespürt werden. Die städtischen Räume mit ihren raffiniert gesetzten architektonischen Raumkanten werden durch Achsen und räumliche Verknüpfungen in Beziehung zueinander gesetzt", lautet die Begründung. „Insgesamt wird die Stadt mit dieser Arbeit um eine Folge subtil verwobener Räume bereichert, die speziell bezogen auf die Schloßinszenierung in der Lage sind, diesem historischen Ort eine räumliche und inhaltliche Bedeutung zu geben."

Das temporäre Holzrahmenbauwerk in den Dimensionen des Schloßes wurde aus finanziellen und inhaltlichen Erwägungen dann allerdings aufgegeben. Auch die reduzierte Inszenierung des früheren Schloßvolumens – ein blauer Kunstrasen mit vier Ecktürmen, die eine Vorstellung von dem Baukörper des Stadtschlosses in der Fläche und in der Höhe erleichtern – wurde nicht realisiert. Lange war umstritten, ob ein Neubau oder eine Rekonstruktion des Schlosses die angemessene Lösung für diesen Ort darstellt. Nach eingehender Diskussion hat die Stadtverordnetenversammlung von Potsdam im Jahr 2000 entschieden, das Schloß wieder aufzubauen. Mit der Errichtung des ehemaligen Hauptzugangs zum Innenhof des Stadtschlosses, des berühmten Fortunaportals, wird ein erstes Zeichen gesetzt.

Der neue Lustgarten ist hingegen schon heute konkret greifbar. Er erstreckt sich von der Anlegestelle der Ausflugsdampfer an der Havel im Osten bis zur Bebauung im Westen und gliedert sich von Norden nach Süden in drei Bereiche: Stadtplatz, Baumhain und Stadtgarten. Bis 1998 wurde das Gelände vom Ernst-Thälmann-Stadion überformt. Der aktuelle Entwurf knüpft sowohl an diese Funktion als Spiel- und Sportstätte wie auch an die historische als Ort des Müßiggangs an.

Der Stadtplatz liegt vor dem historischen Marstall und ist als Ort für Feste und Freizeit konzipiert. Stufenlos gepflastert und mit mobilen Elementen ausgestattet, kann er verschiedenen Veranstaltungen einen angemessenen Rahmen geben und außerdem für Streetball, Skateboarding oder im Winter als Schlittschuhbahn genutzt werden. Wasserschleier auf der Fläche distanzieren optisch und akustisch die Straße vom Stadtgarten. Mit der Baumpflanzung im mittleren Bereich wird ein Filter zwischen Straße und Grünraum geschoben. Im Raster werden fünf Lindenreihen gesetzt, die im Westen als doppelreihige Allee über die gesamte Breite des Gartens fortgeführt wurden. Durch sein 80 Zentimeter höheres Niveau wirkt der Baumhain wie eine Aussichtsplattform, von der eine die gesamte Breite einnehmende Treppe zum Stadtgarten hinunterführt.

Der Stadtgarten ist, anders als die historischen Parks, ein öffentlich nutzbarer Grünraum. Das zentrale Gestaltungselement sind Hecken, die als raumbildende Wand oder Paravent verschiedene Bereiche differenzieren. Nach Süden zur zukünftigen Straßentrasse wird der Grünraum durch ein mit Hopfen beranktes, acht Meter hohes Holzspalier abgeschlossen. Durch klar definierte, thematisch variantenreich ausgebildete Flächen werden vielfältige Nutzungen angeregt. Die Spielfelder für Volley- und Fußball sowie ein Tennisfeld bieten den Rahmen für sportliche Aktivitäten, während Drehsessel und acht Gartenzimmer als kontemplative Orte in Anspruch genommen werden können. Das weitgehend freigelegte Neptunbecken – neben den schon in den sechziger Jahren dorthin translozierten Schloßkolonnaden – ist ein Ort des Verweilens. Die ergänzende Pflanzung von Säuleneichen läßt einen auf sich bezogenen Raum zwischen Anlegestelle und Spielfeldern entstehen, der den Diskontinuitäten seiner Nachbarschaft entrückt zu sein scheint.

Freundschaftsinsel

Das BUGA-Projekt „Freundschaftsinsel" widmet sich den mannigfaltigen Wandlungen der bedeutendsten Potsdamer Gartenanlage des 20. Jahrhunderts. Ihre jeweiligen Gartengestalter, wiewohl sie vom Stil ihrer Epoche geprägt sind, rekrutierten sich stets aus dem Bornimer Kreis um den Staudenzüchter Karl Foerster. Sie arbeiteten einander ergänzend gemäß seinem Diktum, einen „Zusammenklang von Farbe, Formen und Charakteren der Pflanzen" zu erlangen. Eine einmalige Kontinuität liegt in der Person des Gartenarchitekten Hermann Göritz, der 1937, 1953 und 1974 die Pflanzpläne für den Staudengarten erstellte und noch die Anfänge des aktuellen BUGA-Projektes begleitete.

Die gartendenkmalpflegerische Analyse und Konzeption für die von dem in die Havel einmündenden Fluß Nuthe aufgeschwemmte Insel wurde von dem Büro TOPOS Landschaftsplanung, Berlin, erarbeitet. Schwerpunkte waren neben der Rekonstruktion von Teilen früherer Entwürfe und dem Rückbau störender Elemente die Darstellung eines breiten Pflanzenspektrums von Staudenzüchtungen.

Bereits vor zweihundert Jahren wurde die Insel für private Gärten und kleine Werften genutzt. In den dreißiger Jahren des 20. Jahrhunderts führten die Überlegungen der Stadt, hier einen öffentlichen Park anzulegen, sowie Foersters Vorschlag, einen Schau- und Sichtungsgarten in Potsdam zu schaffen, zur ersten Gartenanlage. „Das ganze Blumenzwiebelstaudenreich mit seinen oft in die Tausende gehenden Sortenmengen in ein Dauerverhör zu nehmen." Foerster wollte hier genaue Auskünfte über ideale Wachstumsbedingungen wie etwa Standort, Besonnung oder Verträglichkeit mit anderen Gewächsen erhalten.

Die Anlage, auf deren Grundzüge sich alle folgenden Entwürfe beziehen, entwarf der Gartenarchitekt Hermann

Mattern. Bauliche Fixpunkte sind zwei Torhäuser und die Pergola aus rotem Wesersandstein, die den Garten entlang des nördlichen Ufers begrenzt und durch den „Pappelplatz" mit der heute 150jährigen Baumruine räumlich abgeschlossen wird. Über die Ausführung der Staudenbeete ist durch den beginnenden Krieg wenig bekannt geworden, historische Quellen verzeichnen jedoch in der ersten Hälfte der vierziger Jahre zweitausend Stauden- und hundert Rosenarten.

Bereits 1951 regte Foerster den erneuten Aufbau des durch Krieg und Nutzung als „Grabeland" für die Versorgung der Potsdamer Bevölkerung zerstörten Schau- und Sichtungsgartens auf der Freundschaftsinsel an. Nach Entwürfen von Werner Bauch und Walter Funke wurde von 1953 bis 1957 auf Grundlage Matternscher Gestaltung die Anlage wiederhergestellt und um eine Wasserachse aus fünf Becken mit vier runden Springbrunnen erweitert. Damit konnten auch die von Mattern aus finanziellen Gründen nicht ausgeführten Beete mit Wasser-, Sumpf- und Uferpflanzen präsentiert werden.

Die Umgestaltung anläßlich der X. Weltfestspiele der Jugend 1973 und die 1974 bis 1979 durchgeführte Rekonstruktion des in den fünfziger Jahren angelegten Staudengartens unter Leitung von Funcke und Göritz weist über 80.000 Stauden auf einer Fläche von einem Hektar aus. Zu diesem Anlaß wurde das seit Beginn geplante Café endlich gebaut. Es bildet zusammen mit einem Ausstellungspavillon die räumliche Fassung der Pergola und der Wasserachse. Auch der bereits in den fünfziger Jahren begonnene Rosengarten wurde erheblich erweitert. Zur BUGA Potsdam 2001 werden hier vor allem Rosensorten gezeigt, die während der sechziger und siebziger Jahre in der ehemaligen DDR gezüchtet wurden; sie verschwinden zunehmend aus dem Handel und sollen hier wieder in Erinnerung gerufen werden.

Das botanische Erlebnis zur BUGA ist eine Hommage an Karl Foerster: Aus ganz Europa werden seine Züchtungen zusammengetragen und von Experten auf ihre Echtheit hin gesichtet und bewertet. Neben thematischen Bereichen wie Steingarten und Heidegarten werden in den Beeten parallel zur Pergola über 140 alte, wenig geläufige und aus internationalen Quellen stammende Sammlungen von Taglilien zu sehen sein. Ebenfalls werden verschiedene Sorten der Iris präsentiert, die als „Blume der Friedensgöttin" eine Favoritin Foersters war.

Nuthepark
Der Nuthepark ist eine Anlage im naturnahen Grünraum, die nach dem Entwurf der Berliner Landschaftsarchitekten Fugmann + Janotta neu entstanden ist. Die Uferzone südlich

der Neuen Fahrt wurde erstmals begehbar gemacht und verbindet nun die Stadt entlang der Havel mit dem Schloßpark Babelsberg. An der Mündung der Nuthe in die Havel sind mehrere Orte wie Inseln in dem ehedem nur mit Trampelpfaden durchzogenen Wäldchen angelegt worden, wodurch der urwüchsige Charakter des Gebiets beibehalten werden konnte.

Ein einprägsamer Ort ist die „Lindenhalle": Eine vormals bestehende, doppelreihige Allee wurde von ruderaler Vegetation befreit und als „Naturraum" in Szene gesetzt. In Ost-West-Richtung gelegen, bildet sie das Rückgrat der Gestaltung. Hier ist der Park – ergänzt durch zwei neu angelegte Spielplätze – auch zum Erholungsraum für die Bewohner des benachbarten Wohnquartiers „Zentrum Ost" geworden.

Andere Teile des Parks sind als Biotope nicht zur intensiven Nutzung gedacht, sondern dienen zusammen mit der als Feuchtwiese renaturierten früheren Lagerfläche entlang der Nuthe dem Stadtklima. An der Havel sind an ausgewählten Standorten Holzplattformen über der Uferkante errichtet. Die Besucher dieser Orte werden überrascht von den ungewöhnlichen Prospekten von Süden auf die Stadt oder in die Weite der Havel in Richtung der Glienicker Brücke.

Platz der Einheit
Der Platz der Einheit bildet das Initial zur Wiedergewinnung der früheren Platzanlagen in der Potsdamer Innenstadt. Das Ziel eines Wettbewerbs war ein repräsentativer Stadtplatz, der die geschichtlichen und stadträumlichen Prägungen des Ortes im Kontext der Plätze Potsdams widerspiegelt. Die bis dato dürftige und ungepflegte Anlage sollte eine eigenständige Identität erlangen. Eine besondere Aufgabe war die Integration des Mahnmals für die antifaschistischen Widerstandskämpfer, des Denkmals für den unbekannten Deserteur und ein neu zu errichtendes Denkmal für die ehemalige Synagoge am Platz der Einheit, die in der Pogromnacht 1938 zerstört worden war.

Der einstige Wilhelmplatz gehörte mit Bassinplatz und Plantage zu einer Reihe von Grünräumen, die auf den nicht bebaubaren Resten einer Sumpfrinne angelegt worden waren. „Der mit Linden bepflanzte Platz war während des Siebenjährigen Krieges wieder um einige Fuß tief gesunken und alle Bäume darauf abgestorben. Es mußten daher zur Aufhöhung vierhundertfünfzig Kähne Füllerde angeschafft werden." Dieses Zitat steht für eine prägende Eigenart des Platzes: Bis in die achtziger Jahre des 20. Jahrhunderts sank der Platz immer wieder ab und mußte neu aufgefüllt werden.

Lenné ließ 1831 den Schutt der abgebrannten Nikolaikirche dort verfüllen. Er legte zwei diagonale Wege an, denen er dreißig Jahre später einen Querweg hinzufügte. Am Kreuzungspunkt stand in einem Rondell das Reiterstandbild von Friedrich Wilhelm II. Als 1929 der Platz erneut abgesunken war und wieder aufgefüllt werden mußte, wurde eine einheitliche Rasenfläche angelegt, die bis zur Neugestaltung im Rahmen der BUGA-Vorbereitungen Bestand hatte.

Aus dem Wettbewerb von 1997 ging der Entwurf des Hamburger Büros WES & Partner Landschaftsarchitekten unter der Federführung von Hinnerk Wehberg siegreich hervor. Die Platzgestaltung orientiert sich an dem ersten Entwurf von Lenné. Darüber hinaus gelang dem Gartenarchitekten der überzeugende Verweis auf die Geschichte der stetigen Senkungen, indem er die dreieckigen Flächen zur Mitte hin erhöhte. In dieser Fläche kreuzen sich die auf dem Niveau der Straßen liegenden Wege wie Hohlwege.

Entlang der Wege laden Sitzstufen die Passanten zum beiläufigen Verweilen ein, während Jugendliche Akrobatik auf Skateboards oder mit BMX-Fahrrädern darbieten. Die Lichtinszenierung unterstreicht in der Dunkelheit den skulpturalen Charakter des Platzes und läßt die Ausbildung Wehbergs als Bildhauer ahnen. Die Großform und ihr bestimmendes Wegekreuz aus Sichtbeton erschreckt und fasziniert zugleich – einerseits erscheint vielen die Rohheit des Materials zu ungeschlacht, andererseits überzeugt die Raumbildung zwischen den Stufen. Die bestehenden Denkmäler wurden an ihren Orten belassen, zum Gedenken an die zerstörte Synagoge schlug Wehberg einen Gedenkstein gegenüber ihres früheren Standortes vor.

Der zweite Preis des Wettbewerbs ging an den Zürcher Landschaftsarchitekten Guido Hager. Sein Entwurf knüpft an die Umgestaltung von 1929 an und entwickelt den Platz aus dem Stadtraum. Durch die Baumpflanzungen um die große rechteckige Rasenfläche bildet Hager einen bis zur Langen Brücke hin sichtbaren „Körper". Die Jury schrieb: „Durch das formulierte Entwurfsziel, den Baumhain in den Unterbereichen aufzuasten, wird der Platzraum optisch mit den einzelnen Gebäuden am Platz in Verbindung gebracht, so daß die Intentionen des Stadtplatzes mit denen der Parkanlage verschmelzen. Das Motiv des Wandelns und der Kommunikation in einer Baumhalle wird hier mit Großzügigkeit vorgetragen und bildet einen Rahmen für unterschiedliche Nutzungsansprüche." Die abgesenkte Oberfläche des Rasens und seine strikte Horizontalität assoziieren eine Wasseroberfläche, die lediglich von einer 22 Meter hohen und 13 Meter breiten Glasscheibe zum Gedenken an die zerstörte Synagoge unterbrochen wird.

Mit den Kulissen „Historische Innenstadt" und „Orte am Fluß" stellt die BUGA Potsdam 2001 ein breites Spektrum landschaftsarchitektonischer Positionen vor, die exemplarischen Charakter haben. Die für die jeweiligen Räume erarbeiteten Lösungen bieten bei allem Respekt vor der preußischen Vergangenheit vielfältig nutzbare und vitale Orte. Die getreue Bewahrung bleibt den königlichen Gärten vorbehalten.

Historic City Centre
and Riverside

On leaving the station in Potsdam and setting off towards the centre one is immediately struck by the remains of the historical town silhouette: the dome of the Nikolaikirche, the tower of the Old Town Hall and the long roof of the Marstall (Royal Stables) rise impressively above the Havel. The entrée to the regional capital is indicated by strongly painted façades and the lush green of the river-banks. A summer's day very quickly shows what a positively heavenly enclave Potsdam can represent in Brandenburg's bare "sandpit".

Historische Innenstadt (Historical City Centre) and Orte am Fluss (Riverside) – these names for two of the Horticultural Show venues tell us precisely where they are. Just a few years ago the marks left by the Second World War and the structural consequences of a complete lack of historical awareness combined to give an impression of a desolate urban periphery. Today visitors find themselves standing in the "green centre" of Potsdam. BUGA Potsdam 2001's urban projects pay tribute to the legacy of the last few centuries and cultivate the waterside site. The urban open spaces that once established the identity of the place, but were derelict or had disappeared completely by the early nineties all needed specific design strategies that were both appropriate to modern requirements and can also co-exist with the original royal gardens.

Selected approaches from a spectrum running from re-construction to re-interpretation are available for discussion on the scale of 1:1: the Lustgarten and the Alter Markt, the Freundschaftsinsel, the Nuthepark and the Platz der Einheit. These central open spaces in Potsdam are complemented by the extended Hegelallee promenade, marking the line of the old town wall with squares at the former town gates Nauener Tor and the Jägertor. Part of the town canal, which was filled in in 1961, has been opened up and selected courtyards in the Baroque town centre have been redesigned. The National Horticultural Show Potsdam 2001 has also set parameters for long-term projects like redesigning the Bassinplatz.

As a result of the BUGA town centre projects concentrated on the Havel, people have become more markedly aware of the water in river, canal and little lakes that helped to give Potsdam Island its image in previous centuries. Extending the town to the south has anyway shifted Potsdam's centre of gravity back to the former centre. The decision to build a promenade instead of reconstructing the riverbank develop-ment along the river arm Alte Fahrt means that the individ-ual areas join to form a "green centre". It links up with the open building structures of the fifties and sixties to the north as well as the Potsdam-Center complex that was erect-ed in the nineties around the main station, trying to lend it a correct sense of scale in relation to the town centre.

Lustgarten/Alter Markt

Seen in its Baroque perspective, the route into town via the Lange Brücke ran diagonally towards the Stadtschloss, and then on to the front of the Nikolaikirche, guided by the east façade of the Schloss on one side and the riverside develop-ment at the Alter Markt (Old Market) on the other. The Lust-garten (Pleasance), Potsdam's oldest feudal open space, bordered by colonnades, began between the bridge and the palace.

The brief announced in 1997 for the Lustgarten/Alter Markt competition set a very simple target: regaining the historical space. The empty spaces left by the Stadtschloss and the buildings on the edge of the square caused a loss of tension between the two urban structures that meet at this point. The Nikolaikirche, conceived more as a point de vue within the landscape than within the immediate urban space, was thus brought inappropriately into the foreground.

Admittedly the competition brief was a tough one: it was only possible to offer a temporary solution for the Alter Markt because the tram tracks and road had to be retained, and there was a smouldering debate about the use of and form to be taken by the Stadtschloss site. And in the former Lust-garten area the path to the Mercure hotel, a sixties high-rise building, and the inner-city ring road planned parallel with the railway line were firmly fixed parameters.

The jury's unanimous vote was to award the first prize to the group made up of freiRaum. Planungsgruppe Stadt Garten Landschaft and Dietz Joppien Architekten. This deci-sion was a tribute to the convincing nature of a design that untied the Gordian knot in this sensitive area, rather than cutting it. "The project distinguishes itself by using clear structures to trace the historical spatial sequences. The ur-ban spaces, edged with subtly placed architecture, are related to each other by axes and spatial links," wrote the jury.

"The town as a whole will be enhanced by a sequence of subtly interlinked spaces as a result of this work, which by its presentation of the Stadtschloss in particular is able to give this historical place some meaning in terms of space and content."

In fact, the temporary wood skeleton structure in the dimensions of the Stadtschloss was abandoned for financial reasons, and because of its potential implications. Ideas for a presentation of the Schloss – reduced to a blue artificial lawn and four corner towers representing the building volume by way of its surface and in its hight – were not realized, either. There was controversy for a long time about whether a new building or a reconstruction of the Schloss would be the appropriate solution for this site. After detailed discussions the Potsdam town council decided in 2000 to rebuild the Schloss. A first sign will be set when the former main entrance to the inner courtyard, the famous Fortuna Portal, is erected.

In contrast with this, the new Lustgarten is perfectly tangible already today. It extends from the landing stage for steamer trips on the Havel in the east to the building development in the west, and is structured as three areas from north to south: municipal square, grove of trees and municipal gardens. The site was dominated by the Ernst Thälmann Stadium until 1998. The current design links up with this function as a venue for games and sport, and with the historical function as a place for spending leisure time.

The municipal square in front of the historic Marstall is intended for fairs and leisure. It is paved, without steps, and fitted with mobile units, thus offering an appropriate framework for various events, and also available for street ball games, skateboarding or as a skating rink in winter. Veils of water on the paved expanse distance the road from the municipal gardens visually and acoustically. A filter is placed between the street and the green open space by the trees planted in the central area. Five rows of limes are placed in a grid, and this is continued in a double avenue running across the full breadth of the gardens. Because it is 80 centimetres higher, the grove of trees seems like a viewing platform from which a flight of steps occupying the full width leads down to the municipal gardens.

The municipal gardens, unlike the historical parks, are a green space that can be used by the public. Hedges form the central design element, distinguishing various areas as space-defining walls or screens. On the south side, where the road is intended to run in future, the green area will be bounded by an eight metre high wooden trellis with hops growing up it. Clearly defined and thematically varied areas will encourage a wide range of uses. The volleyball courts and football pitches and a tennis court offer venues for sporting activities, while movable armchairs and eight gar-

den rooms can be used as places for sitting quietly and thinking. The Neptune Basin – along with the Schloss colonnades, which were relocated here in the sixties – has been largely opened up, and is intended to provide a pleasant place in which to spend time doing nothing. The additional planting of cypress oaks creates a self-referential space between the landing-stage and the playing fields, which seems far removed from its fragmented neighbourhood.

Freundschaftsinsel

The Freundschaftsinsel (Friendship Island) project is devoted to the many and various transformations that Potsdam's most important 20th century garden has undergone. The garden designers who have worked on it, although all steeped in the style of their own epochs, were always recruited from the Bornim circle that formed around Karl Foerster, who was a breeder of herbaceous plants. They worked by complementing each other, on the basis of his dictum that "harmony of colour, form and plant character" should be the aim. Unique continuity is provided by the person of landscape gardener Hermann Göritz, who drew up the planting schemes for the herbaceous garden in 1937, 1953 and 1974, and was even involved in the early stages of the current project.

The analysis and concept in terms of garden preservation for this island washed together by the river Nuthe, a tributary of the Havel, was devised by the office of TOPOS Landschaftsplanung, Berlin. Its main aim was to present a broad spectrum of herbaceous plants, as well as reconstruct parts of earlier designs and remove elements that were out of place.

As many as two hundred years ago the island was used for private gardens and little boat-building operations. In the 1920s, the town's ideas for establishing a public park here and Foerster's suggestion that a specimen garden should be created in Potsdam led to the first experiment: "putting the whole range of herbaceous plants grown from bulbs, with its varieties often numbering thousands, into a state of perpetual interrogation." Foerster's aim was to acquire precise information about ideal growing conditions like for example location, sunlight or compatibility with other plants.

The garden that forms the basis for all subsequent designs was created by landscape gardener Hermann Mattern. Two gatehouses and the pergola built of red Weser sandstone border the garden on the north bank, concluding the "Poplar Square" with its tree ruin, now 150 years old. Little is known about how the herbaceous beds turned out because of the war that was just starting, but historical sources record two thousand herbaceous varieties and a hundred varieties of roses in the early forties.

As early as 1951 Foerster was proposing the restorations of the specimen garden on the Freundschaftsinsel, which had been destroyed by the war and by being designated as available to the people of Potsdam for cultivating food. The garden was restored from 1953 to 1957 according to designs by Werner Bauch and Walter Funke, which were based on Mattern's concept, and extended by the addition of a water axis made up of five basins with four round fountains. This meant that the beds featuring water, marsh and bank plants that Mattern had not been able to complete for financial reasons could be realized.

The new design introduced on the occasion of the X World Youth Festival in 1973 and the reconstruction of the herbaceous garden created by Funcke and Göritz in the fifties identifies over 80,000 herbaceous plants in an area of one hectare. Eventually the café that had been planned from the outset was built on this occasion. The café and an exhibition pavilion provide a spatial framework for the pergola and the water axis. The rose garden that was started in the fifties was also considerably extended. This will be used at the National Horticultural Show particularly to show rose varieties that were cultivated in the sixties and seventies in the former GDR; they are increasingly disappearing from the market and are now to be brought back to people's attention.

The botanical event is a homage to Karl Foerster: plants he cultivated will be brought together from all over Europe and examined and evaluated by experts to assess how authentic they are. There will be themed areas like rock gardens and heather gardens, and over 140 old, relatively unfamiliar day-lilies from international sources will be shown in the beds running parallel with the pergola. Various varieties of iris will also be shown, a favourite of Foerster's as the "flower of the goddess of peace".

Nuthepark

The Nuthepark is a feature of the semi-natural open space created to a design by the Berlin landscape architects Fugmann + Janotta. The banks south of the river arm Neue Fahrt were first of all restored to take footpaths, and now link the town with the Babelsberg Schlosspark via a riverside walk. At the confluence of the Nuthe and the Havel there are several places where islands have been formed in the little woods that only had rough paths beaten through them, which means that the natural character of the area could be retained.

One striking place is the Lime Hall: a double avenue that had existed previously was cleared of ruderal vegetation and presented as a "natural space". It runs from east to west, and forms the spine of the design. Here the park – completed by the addition of two new playgrounds – is also a place where residents of the neighbouring Zentrum Ost residential area can relax.

Other parts of the park are biotopes that are not just intended for intensive use, but help to enhance the climate of the town, together with the former storage area along the Nuthe, which has been restored as a water-meadow. Wooden platforms have been erected in selected places above the edge of the banks along the Havel. Visitors to these places will be surprised by the unusual views from the south of the town or across the wide Havel towards the Glienicker Brücke.

Platz der Einheit

The Platz der Einheit (Unity Square) is the initial step in restoring the former public squares in central Potsdam. The competition was aiming at a prestigious municipal square reflecting the place's history and urban development in the context of Potsdam's squares. To date the complex has been poor and uncared for, and was to acquire an identity of its own. Particular features of the brief were to integrate the memorial to the anti-Fascist resistance fighter, the monument to the unknown deserter and a new monument to mark the site of the former synagogue in the Platz der Einheit, which was destroyed in the pogrom night of 1938.

The former Wilhelmplatz, including the Bassinplatz, a square with a pool, and the so-called plantation was one of a series of green spaces that had been established on the remains of a marsh drainage channel on which it had not been possible to build. "This square planted with lime trees had sunk again by a number of feet during the Seven Years' War and all the trees in it had died. Thus four hundred and fifty barges of soil had to be brought in to raise it." This quotation identifies one of the square's key features: until the eighties it kept subsiding and had to be filled in again.

Lenné had the rubble from the Nikolaikirche, which had burned down, taken there as a filler in 1831. He laid two diagonal paths, to which he added a transverse route thirty years later. The equestrian statue of Friedrich Wilhelm II stood in a roundel at the point of intersection. When the square had sunk again in 1929 and had to be filled in again, a uniform lawn was laid that remained until the area was redesigned as part of the preparations for the National Horticultural Show.

The 1997 competition was won by a design from the Hamburg office of WES & Partner Landschaftsarchitekten, with Hinnerk Wehberg in charge. The design for the square is based on Lenné's first design. As well as this, the landscape gardener was able to refer convincingly to the story of the constant sinking by raising the triangular areas towards the centre. The paths at street level cross at this point like sunken lanes.

Beside the paths are steps for sitting on, inviting passers-by to stop and relax casually, while young people provide acrobatic displays on skateboards or BMX bikes. The lighting enhances the sculptural effect of the square after dark, and gives an inkling of Wehberg's training as a sculptor. The large-scale form and the cross at the intersection of the paths in exposed concrete that is its defining feature is both alarming and fascinating – some people find the raw quality of the material too massive and ungainly, but the way space is created between the steps is convincing. The existing monuments are left in place, and Wehberg proposes a memorial stone opposite the former site of the destroyed synagogue.

The second prize in the competition went to the Zurich landscape architect Guido Hager. His idea took up the 1929 refurbishment and developed the square from the urban space. Hager creates a "body" that is visible through the plantations of trees around the large rectangular lawn as far as the Lange Brücke. The jury wrote: "The stated aim of the design to lop the lower areas of the grove of trees links the square visually with the individual buildings in the square, so that the intentions of the municipal square blend with those of the park. The motif of change and communication in a tree hall is presented generously here and forms a framework for the various uses to which the square will be put." The sunken surface of the lawn and its strictly horizontal quality suggest a sheet of water, broken only by the 22 metre high and 13 metre wide pane of glass in memory of the destroyed synagogue.

The National Horticultural Show presents a broad spectrum of approaches to landscape architecture that are exemplary in character in the settings of the Historical City Centre and the Riverside. The solutions devised for the various areas create lively spaces that could be used in a variety of ways, while respecting the Prussian past. Faithful preservation is left to the royal gardens.

❶

❶ Die Inszenierung am Alten Markt – mit Grabungsfeldern und Ecktürmen – sollte die aktuellen Verkehrstrassen überlagern und den Standort des einstigen Stadtschlosses markieren; im Hintergrund ist die 2000 begonnene Rekonstruktion des Fortunaportals eingetragen.

The presentation in the Old Market – with archaeological excavations and corner towers – was to be superimposed on the present roads and to mark the site of the former Stadtschloss; the reconstruction of the Fortuna Portal, which started in 2000, is seen in the background.

❷ Die in einem Wettbewerb prämierte räumliche Inszenierung des Stadtschlosses wurde aus finanziellen und inhaltlichen Erwägungen aufgegeben.

The three-dimensional presentation of the Stadtschloss, winner of a competition, was abandoned for financial and conceptual reasons.

❸ Der Wettbewerbsentwurf überzeugte durch das Aufspüren der historischen Raumfolgen.

This competition design convinced by tracking down the historical organization of the space.

2

...en- und Realisierungswettbewerb für Landschaftsarchitekten und Architekten/ Stadtplaner, Potsdam - Lustgarten / Alter Markt 1997, 2. Stufe

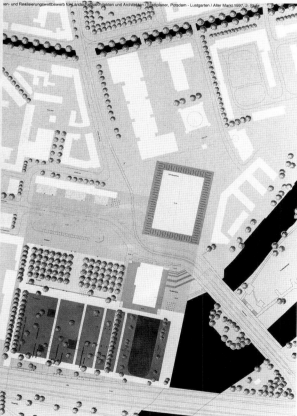

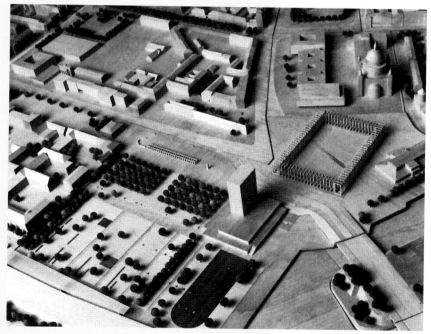

3

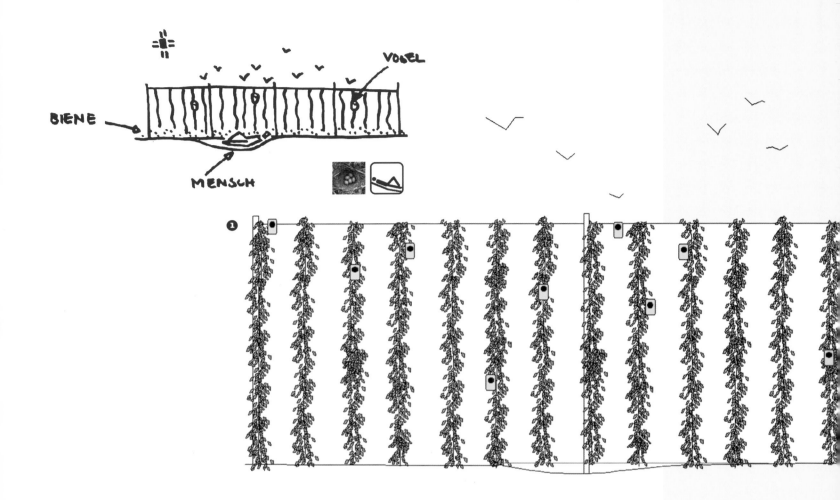

VOGEL

BIENE

MENSCH

❶ Eine hohe Hopfengalerie begrenzt den neuen Lustgarten nach Süden zur zukünftigen Entlastungsstraße und zur Bahntrasse.

A high hop gallery borders the new Lustgarten on the south side, facing the planned ring road and the railway line.

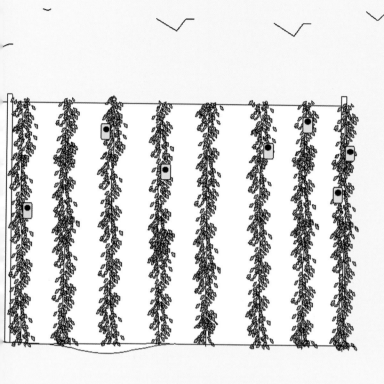

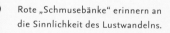 Rote „Schmusebänke" erinnern an die Sinnlichkeit des Lustwandelns.

Red „lovers' benches" evoke the sensuality of strolling.

❸ Noch bedarf es einiger Vorstellungskraft, sich den grünen Baumfilter zwischen der Breiten Straße und der Spielfäche im Süden vorzustellen.

It still needs a little imagination to picture the green filter of trees between the Breite Strasse and the play area in the south.

❶ Wie eine kleine Oase liegt der Heckengarten inmitten der Rasenfläche.

The hedge garden is placed in the middle of the lawn like a little oasis

❷ Mit kleinen Rampen soll die Skater-Szene Potsdams auf den planen Platz gelockt werden.

Potsdam's skateboard scene is to be lured to the flat square with small-scale ramps.

❸ Der Prospekt auf die Stadt zeigt die breite Treppenanlage, die vom Stadtniveau auf das Gartenlevel herabführt.

The view of the town shows the broad flight of steps leading from the town level down to the level of the gardens.

❹ Die an die Formensprache der sechziger Jahre erinnernden Sessel lassen sich nach der Sonne ausrichten.

These chairs, reminiscent of the formal language of the sixties, can be adjusted according to the position of the sun.

❺ Im Neptunbecken sind nur wenige Teile der Skulptur erhalten, die einst das Bassin hinter dem Stadtschloß berühmt machte.

Only a few items of sculpture in the Neptune Fountain that once brought fame to the basin behind the Stadtschloss have survived.

②

③

④

⑤

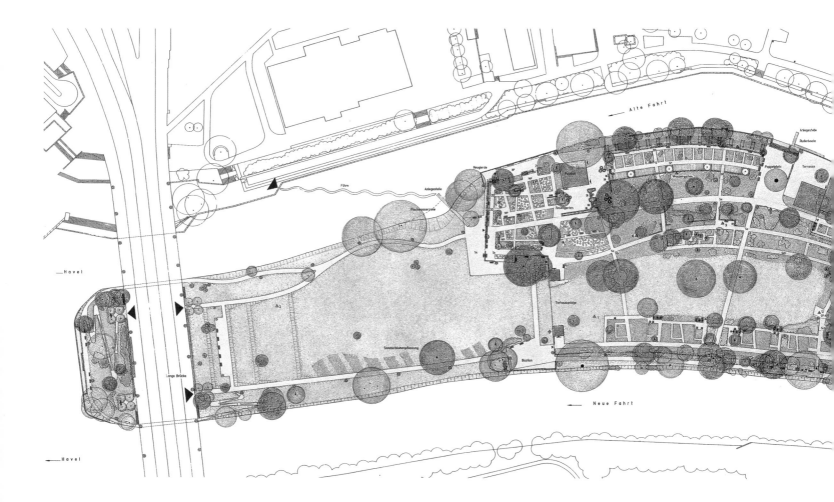

❶ Im Mittelpunkt der Konzeption für die Freundschaftsinsel steht die Rekonstruktion und Erneuerung des Stauden- und Sichtungsgartens. Im Osten der Insel wurden ein Spielplatz und eine Arena vorgesehen (nur teilweise realisiert).

Reconstructing the herbaceous and specimen garden is central to the concept for Friendship Island. A playground and an arena in the eastern part were only partially realized.

❷ Zwei Torhäuser markierten von Anbeginn die Zugänge zum eingefriedeten Garten.

Two gatehouses marked the access points to the enclosed garden from the outset.

❸ Die Freundschaftsinsel bildet eine Art Central Park in Stadtgebiet von Potsdam.

Friendship Island is a kind of Central Park in the city of Potsdam.

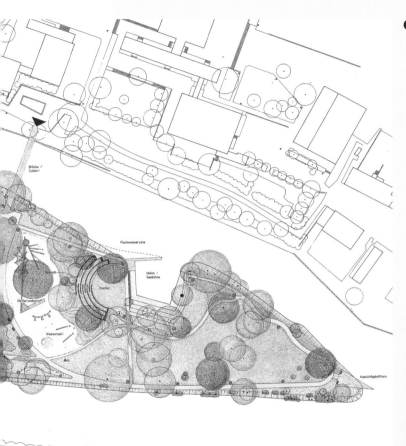

1

Brücke / Zufahrt

Flachwasserzone

Hafen / Seebühne

Theater

Kletterlandschaft

Wasserspiel

Aussichtsplattform

→ Havel

3

2

❶ Der Pflanzplan für ein Beet weist auf die Vielfältigkeit der Staudenzüchtungen hin, die hier ausgestellt werden.

The planting plan for each bed indicates the very wide range of herbaceous varieties that are to be shown here.

❷ Die gartendenkmalpflegerische Konzeption zeigt die verschiedenen Zeitschichten, die in der Folge der Ideen Karl Foersters und ihrer Weiterentwicklung durch den Bornimer Kreis entstanden sind.

The garden monument conservation concept shows the various time strata that emerged as a result of Karl Foerster's ideas and their further development by the Bornim Circle.

❸ Die von Hermann Mattern entworfene Pergola, die bereits Teil des ersten Gartens war, wurde anläßlich der BUGA Potsdam 2001 wieder in ihren Originalzustand versetzt.

The pergola designed by Hermann Mattern was part of the first garden and was restored to its original state for the National Horticultural Show.

❶

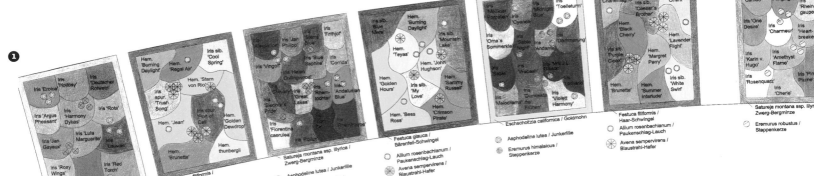

❸

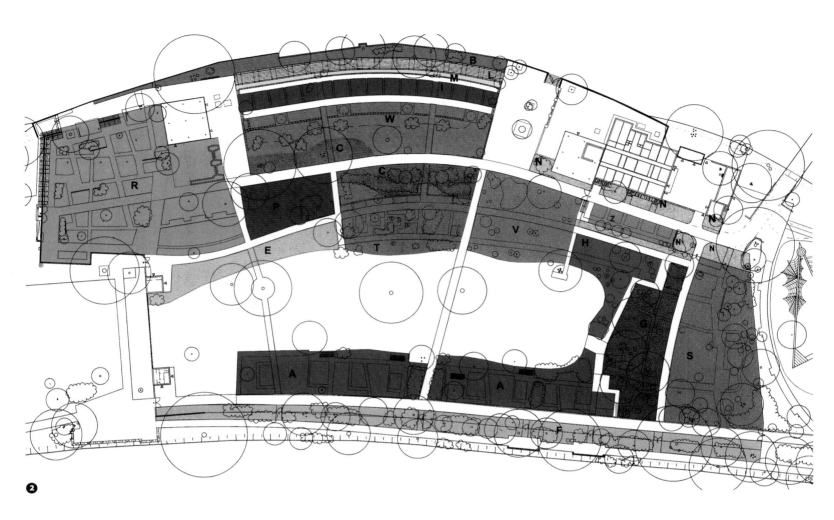

R	Rosengarten nach Funcke 7oer Jahre
B	Blattschmuckstauden nach Mattern 3oer Jahre, nach Funcke und Göritz 5oer Jahre
M	Staudenrabatte nach Funcke und Göritz 5oer Jahre
L	Kletterpflanzen nach Göritz überwiegend 3oer Jahre
I	Iris- und Tagliliengarten nach Göritz 5oer Jahre
W	Wasser-, Sumpf- und Uferrandpflanzen nach Funcke und Göritz 5oer Jahre
C	Schattenstauden nach Göritz 5oer und 7oer Jahre
P	Pfingstrosen mit Stauden nach Göritz 7oer Jahre
T	Steingarten nach Göritz 5oer Jahre, nach Funcke und Altmann 5oer bis 7oer Jahre, nach Näthe 8oer Jahre

E	Prachtstaudenrabatte nach Göritz 7oer Jahre
V	Staudenverwendung nach Göritz 5oer Jahre
H	Heidegarten nach Göritz 5oer Jahre
Z	Kräutergarten nach Näthe 8oer Jahre
G	Gräser und Bodendecker nach Funcke 7oer Jahre
S	Schatten-, Halbschatten- und Blattschmuckstauden nach Funcke 7oer Jahre
F	Vorfrühlings- und Frühlingsblüher nach Göritz 5oer und 7oer Jahre
N	Neuanlage
A	Karl-Foerster-Staudenzüchtungen

Freundschaftsinsel

Zentrum Ost

❸

❹

❶ Die Kastenbrücke über die Nuthe verbindet die Uferpromenaden.

The box-girder bridge over the river Nuthe links the embankment promenades.

❷ Die Atmosphäre entlang der Neuen Fahrt wird bestimmt durch die Weite der Havel und das grüne Ufer, die in reizvollem Kontrast zu Merkzeichen wie dem Heilig-Geist-Spital stehen.

The broad sweep of the Havel and the green bank give the river arm Neue Fahrt its particular atmosphere, forming a charming contrast with landmarks like the Heilig-Geist-Spital.

❸ Ein Spielplatz verknüpft den Park mit dem Wohnquartier „Zentrum Ost".

A playground links the park with the Zentrum Ost residential district.

❹ Der Übersichtsplan zeigt die Promenade zwischen der Langen Brücke und dem Schloßpark Babelsberg, die sich auf beiden Seiten der Nuthemündung zu einem Park aufweitet.

This outline plan shows the promenade between the Lange Brücke and the Babelsberg Schlosspark, which opens up into a park on both sides of the mouth of the Nuthe.

❶ Der Wilhelmplatz nach dem Entwurf Lennés von 1862 wird durch die diagonale Wegeführung charakterisiert, hier gezeichnet vom späteren Berliner Gartenbaudirektor Gustav Meyer.

Wilhelmplatz, designed by Lenné in 1862, has characteristic diagonal paths, drawn here by Gustav Meyer, who later became Berlin's director of horticulture.

❷ Der Entwurf von Hinnerk Wehberg (in WES & Partner) für den heutigen Platz der Einheit orientiert sich an der historischen Vorlage und thematisiert gleichzeitig das mehrmalige Absacken des Baugrunds.

The design by Hinnerk Wehberg (in WES & Partner) for what is now Unity Square draws on the historical model and at the same time addresses the fact that the land sank on several occasions.

❸ Der Blick auf der Ostseite des Wilhelmplatzes zur Nikolaikirche um 1940 zeigt die Synagoge auf der linken Seite des Platzes (vor dem Postamt).

The view on the east side of Wilhelmplatz towards the Nikolaikirche in about 1940 shows the synagogue on the left-hand side of the square (in front of the post office).

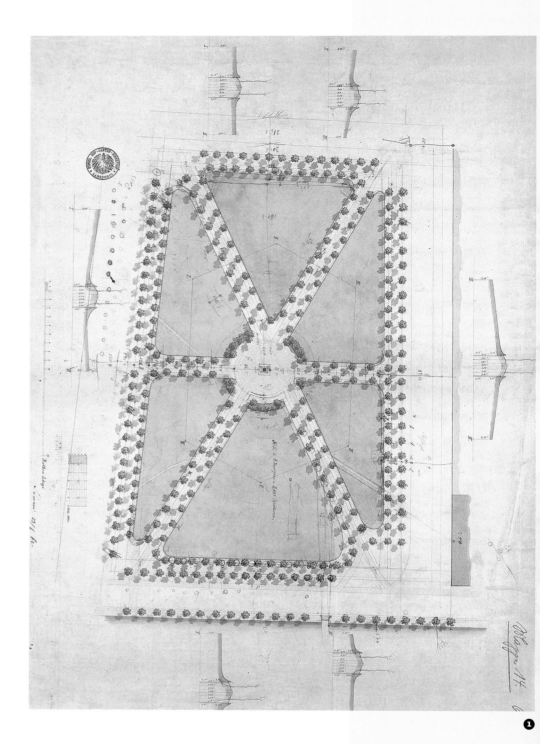

❶

3

2

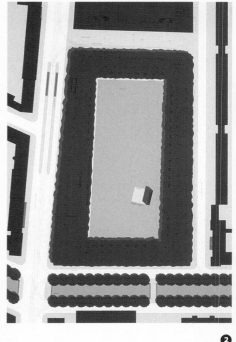

1

2

3

4

1 Der Wilhelmplatz 1936 nach der
Aufgabe der Lennéschen Gestaltung.

**Wilhelmplatz in 1936, when the de-
sign by Lenné had been abandoned.**

2 Der Entwurf von Guido Hager sieht
ebenfalls eine homogene Rasenfläche vor.

**The design by Guido Hager also
opts for the lawn as a homoge-
neous surface.**

3 Das Wegekreuz im Platz der Einheit
läßt durch die zwischen den Stufen
gepflanzten Bäume ein reizvolles,
an barocke Parks erinnerndes Vexier-
spiel zwischen Mensch und Pflanze
entstehen.

**The trees planted between the steps
at the point where the paths cross
in Unity Square creates a charming,
puzzle-like interplay of plants and
man, reminiscent of Baroque parks.**

4 Die Baumreihen um die Grünfläche
definieren den Platz zu einem
eigenständigen öffentlichen
Stadtraum.

**The rows of trees around the green
area make the square into a public
space in its own right.**

Essay von **Guido Hager**

Über den zeitgemäßen Umgang mit historischen Gärten

Für einen Garten wäre es das beste, wenn er über Jahrzehnte, Jahrhunderte gleichmäßig gepflegt und unterhalten wird. Dies ist aber selten der Fall. Wann immer nach den schönsten alten Gärten gefragt wird, werden jene Beispiele genannt, die erst kürzlich mit einem großen Aufwand in ihren ursprünglichen Zustand zurückversetzt wurden. Oft wird dabei vergessen, daß diese Gärten zwar auf einem historischen Plan ähnlich aussehen, vielleicht auch auf gefundenen Fundamenten aufbauen, aber eigentlich neue Gärten in einem alten Gewand sind.

Auch bei einigen innerstädtischen Grünräumen in Potsdam, wo eine Rekonstruktion nach Jahrzehnte währender Abwesenheit des Originals fragwürdig ist, sollten alternative Konzepte für den Umgang mit historischen Gärten diskutiert werden. In der Charta von Venedig aus dem Jahr 1964 liest man unter Artikel 9, daß „die Restaurierung einen Ausnahmecharakter behalten" solle und da aufhöre, wo die Hypothese beginnt. Darüber hinaus soll sich jede als unerläßlich anerkannte Ergänzung „von der architektonischen Komposition unterscheiden und den Stempel unserer Zeit tragen". In der spezifisch auf den Garten bezogenen Charta von Florenz aus dem Jahr 1981 steht in Artikel 16: „Rekonstruktionen kommen gelegentlich in Partien in Frage, die in unmittelbarer Nähe eines Gebäudes liegen." Artikel 21 führt weiter aus, daß „mit Unterhaltsmaßnahmen oder konservierenden Eingriffen die Authentizität des Gartens wiederzugewinnen" sei. Authentizität heißt zu deutsch: Echtheit. Authentizität aber ist wiederzugewinnen, indem Altem Neues zugefügt oder entgegengesetzt wird.

Seit meinem ersten Auftrag setze ich mich mit historischen Gärten auseinander. Die Beschäftigung mit der Denkmaltheorie lehrte mich, daß wir in einem Garten historische Elemente bestimmen und erhalten, nicht aber historische Elemente durch Rekonstruktion neu erschaffen können. Selbstverständlich arbeitete ich vor allem daran, Überkommenes zu erhalten und wo immer nötig zu konservieren, am liebsten über eine langfristige Pflege. Wo es jedoch wenig zu erhalten gibt, ergänze ich das Gartendenkmal – mit zeitgenössischer Gestaltung. Dadurch wird dem Gartendenkmal der Alterswert nicht streitig gemacht. Aber der Umgang mit einem historischen Garten wird wieder zum gestalterischen Akt qualifiziert.

In der Baudenkmalpflege ist die Rekonstruktion von bereits verlorenen Bauwerken verpönt. Dagegen gehört die Weiterentwicklung historischer Bauten zum Alltag, man denke an die Bauten von Karljosef Schattner in der Altstadt von Eichstätt. In der Gartendenkmalpflege dagegen ist die Rekonstruktion Usus. Trauen wir uns keine Zukunft der Landschaftsarchitektur zu? Oder verleitet der Mangel an ständiger Pflege dazu, immer wieder den Originalzustand herstellen zu wollen? Doch was ist eigentlich der Originalzustand eines alten Gartens?

Zwei Beispiele sollen erklären, was ich meine. Das erste, der Rechberggarten, dient als Ort der Entspannung mitten in der Stadt, ein schöner Zier- und Nutzgarten, der uns etwas vom alten Zürich erzählt und von den hier wechselnden Gartenmoden. Er ist einer der prächtigsten Barockgärten der Stadt aus der zweiten Hälfte des 18. Jahrhunderts und wurde seit seiner Erstellung oft umgestaltet. Seit 1985 ist der ganze Garten der Öffentlichkeit zugänglich gemacht worden. Das Projekt beläßt sowohl die letzten barocken Elemente als auch die mit der ersten Umgestaltung um 1840 ausgeführten Terrainveränderungen und auch jene der vereinfachten Rekonstruktion von 1938. Die wichtigen Mauern, Wiesenböschungen und Bäume wurden als originale Substanz der verschiedenen Bauetappen geschützt und saniert. Zusätzliche Einbauten und Pflanzungen ergänzen den Garten nach historischem Vorbild in zeitgenössischer Sprache. Seit der Mauersanierung 1992 wachsen in den buchsgefaßten Beeten Birnen- und Weichselspaliere. Das zentrale Parterre ist als Blumenstück neu bepflanzt. Eine lange, üppige Blumenrabatte schmückt die erste Hauptterrasse. Der Wechselflor wird jährlich anders zusammengestellt, sei es nach historischen Vorbildern oder mit heutigem Pflanzenmaterial. „Das Vorhandene stärken und mit Neuem anreichern" könnte das Motto zu diesem Projekt heißen.

Ein anderes Beispiel für die Überlagerung von Substanz und neuen Anforderungen ist der Garten der Villa Bleuler, deren unter Schutz gestellte Gartenanlage sich seit Beginn der achtziger Jahre im Besitz der Stadt Zürich befindet. Mit dem Einzug des Schweizerischen Instituts für Kunstwissenschaft mußte eine Bibliothek unter dem Rasenrondell eingebaut werden, was aus gartendenkmalpflegerischer Sicht falsch ist, politisch jedoch nicht verhindert werden konnte. Die natürliche Belichtung der unterirdischen Bibliothek mittels Oberlicht und Fenstern in der Stützmauer wurde hingegen aus gartendenkmalpflegerischer Sicht unterstützt. Als zentraler Ort innerhalb des neuen Baukomplexes bleibt so die Bibliothek sowohl von innen als auch von außen als ein Teil der Komposition sicht- und spürbar. Das Oberlicht und die Fenster sind in ihrer Spannung zur vorhandenen und rekonstruierten Substanz Faktoren der Verunsicherung, die es braucht, damit keine heile Welt vorgetäuscht und der Garten nicht zum nostalgischen Kitsch gemindert wird. Die Alterspatina, die die Atmosphäre des Gartens ausmacht, wird durch das Moos an den dicken Stämmen, die waldartige Vegetation unter den großen Bäumen oder die dicke weiche Kiesschicht bestimmt. Mit der Sanierung wurden bewußt Spuren des Vergehens, eine Besonderheit des alten Gartens, erhalten. Den Staudenrabatten wurde erhöhte Aufmerksamkeit geschenkt: Sie spiegeln etwas von der Üppigkeit der gärtnerischen Aufwendungen im villennahen Bereich wider.

Die künftige Weitergestaltung muß bei jeder gartendenkmalpflegerischen Aufgabe gleichwertig mitdiskutiert werden. Für die sich ergebende Interpretationsfülle braucht es Auftraggeber und Fachleute, die bereit sind, sich auf das Wagnis mit dem Vergänglichen einzulassen. Mit jedem Zufügen entstehen natürlich Brüche zwischen dem Alten und dem Neuen. Doch unsere Welt ist voll von Brüchen, und wir müssen sie auch im historischen Park kultivieren – ohne dabei den Park als Ganzes aus den Augen zu verlieren. Der Park soll nicht zu einer Ansammlung von Brüchen werden, sondern zu einem neuen, wenn auch heterogenen Ganzen.

Zu oft muß als Legitimation für die Arbeit am Gartendenkmal ein unreflektierter Vorher- und Nachher-Effekt her, der über das schlechte Vorher und das gute Nachher geschaffen wird. Dieser ist mit einer Rekonstruktion zwar einfacher herzustellen als mit einem Abwägen zwischen Erhalten und Weitergestalten. Doch dabei verliert der Garten seine Glaubwürdigkeit, wenn das scheinbar Alte nicht alt ist. Das Ergebnis: Alt und Neu sind nicht mehr zu unterscheiden, und das Gartendenkmal verliert das, was ihm eigen ist: das Gewachsene. Als Kulturleistung unserer Tage gilt es, alte Gärten im neuen Gewand zu gestalten. Orte, die altern können und die das erreichen, was wir an alten Gärten lieben: eine Stimmung zu haben und nicht auf Stimmung zu machen.

Guido Hager leitet das Landschaftsarchitekturbüro Hager AG in Zürich.

Essay by **Guido Hager**

Advanced work with historical gardens

Ideally a garden would be tended and maintained continually for decades, for centuries. But this is seldom the case. Whenever people ask about the finest old gardens, the examples mentioned are those that have been recently restored to their original condition, involving a great deal of effort and expense. What is often forgotten is that these gardens look similar on a historical plan, and are perhaps also building on existing foundations, but actually they are new gardens in old garments.

There are some inner-city green spaces in Potsdam as well where a reconstruction of the original would be dubious after decades of absence, and here alternative concepts for dealing with historical gardens should be discussed. In the 1964 Charter of Venice, Article 9 states that "restoration (should) retain exceptional character" and should stop "where hypothesis begins". Beyond this, any addition that is seen as essential should "be distinct from the architectural composition and carry the stamp of our times." Article 16 of the 1981 Charter of Florence, which relates specifically to gardens, states: "Reconstructions are occasionally acceptable in areas that are very close to a building." Article 21 mentions that "the authenticity of the garden (is) to be regained by maintenance measures or interventions intended to conserve". But authenticity can be regained by adding new to old, or by setting them in contrast with each other.

I have been dealing with historical gardens since my first commission. My study of monument theory taught me that we identify and maintain historical elements in a garden, but cannot re-create historical elements by reconstruction. Of course I work above all on maintaining what has come down to us, and conserving it wherever necessary, ideally by long-term care. But where there is little to maintain, I complement the garden monument – with contemporary design. This does not place the value of the garden as an ancient monument in question. But dealing with a historical garden then acquires the quality of a creative act.

Reconstructing buildings that have already been lost is frowned upon in the world of monument preservation and the alternative, developing historical buildings further, is an everyday event – think of Karljosef Schattner's buildings in the old town in Eichstätt. But reconstruction is customary in historical garden preservation. Do we have no confidence in the future of landscape architecture? Or does the lack of constant care tempt us into wanting to restore gardens to their original condition? But what actually is the original condition of an old garden?

I will give two examples to explain what I mean. The first, the Rechberg Garden, is a place of relaxation in the town centre, a beautiful decorative and productive garden that tells us something about old Zurich and the way garden fashions have changed. It is one of the city's most splendid Baroque gardens dating from the second half of the 18th century, and has often been redesigned since it was created. The whole garden has been open to the public since 1985. The project keeps both the last of the Baroque elements and also the changes of terrain that were carried out for the first new design around 1840, and also those introduced in the simplified reconstruction of 1938. The important walls, banks of lawn and trees were protected and restored as original stock from the various construction phases. Additional structures and planting complete the garden on the historical model, but using contemporary language. Espalier pears and sour cherries have been grown in the box-framed beds since the walls were refurbished in 1992. The central bed has been replanted as a flower feature. The first main terrace is decorated with a long, luxuriant flower border. The bedding-out plants are put together differently each year, either following a historical pattern or using modern plants. "Reinforcing what is already there and enriching it with modern additions," could be the motto for this project.

Another example of features that are already in place and new demands overlapping is provided by the Villa Bleuler, whose listed gardens have been owned by the city of Zurich since the early eighties. When the Swiss Institute of Art History moved in, a library had to be installed under the lawn roundel, which is wrong in terms of historical garden preservation, but could not be prevented politically. Yet the natural lighting of the underground library from a skylight and windows in the supporting wall was endorsed from the point of view of historical garden preservation. In this way the library, as a central place within the new building complex, remains visible and tangible as part of the composition. The skylight and the windows are in a state of tension with the existing and reconstructed features, and provide the uncertainty factors that are needed to avoid simulating a perfect world and reducing the garden to a piece of nostalgic kitsch. The patina of age that establishes the atmosphere of the garden is created by the moss on the thick trunks, the wood-like vegetation under the big trees or the thick soft layer of gravel. The refurbishment deliberately retained traces of transience, a special feature of the old garden. Particular attention was paid to the herbaceous borders: they reflect something of the lavish quality of the expenditure that has been made on the gardens of the nearby villas.

The potential for a continuous design process must be discussed on an equal footing for every piece of historical garden maintenance. If the desired richness of interpretation is to be achieved, clients and experts are needed who are ready to take risks with transient things. Of course every addition creates breaks between the old and the new. But our world is full of breaks, and we must also cultivate them in historic parks – without losing sight of the park as a whole. The park should not become an accumulation of breaks, but a new, if heterogeneous whole.

Too often a thoughtless "before and after" effect is used to legitimize work on a historic garden, created by a bad before and a good after. This is certainly easier to achieve by reconstruction rather than by weighing maintenance up against creating something new. But the garden will lose its credibility if something that seems to be old is not old. The result: old and new can no longer be distinguished, and the historic garden loses its particular quality: the fact that it has grown. Our task today is to create old gardens in new garments, places that can age and achieve something that we love about old gardens: having an atmosphere, rather than pretending to have an atmosphere.

Guido Hager is head of Hager AG landscape architecture practice in Zurich, Switzerland.

Gartenschau – Show und Chance

Könige und Kaiser haben Potsdam schon lange verlassen. Manche Kritiker wollen glauben machen, daß diese Herrschenden den Anspruch, schöne Gärten und gute Architektur zu schaffen, mit sich genommen haben. Doch auch demokratische Staaten und Städte sind sich ihrer Aufgabe für öffentlichen Raum und Stadtgestalt zumeist bewußt. Um jedoch große finanzielle und politische Kraftanstrengungen im Maßstab einstiger monarchischer Anlagen unternehmen zu können, bedienen sich die Städte heute eines übergeordneten Festivals.

Beispiele für solche Veranstaltungen gibt es nicht nur im Bereich der Landschaftsarchitektur und Gartenkunst. Neben Weltausstellungen oder Olympischen Spielen werden auch Bauausstellungen wie die Interbau 1957 in Berlin, die mit dem Hansaviertel den Zukunftsanspruch des westlichen Teils der Stadt demonstrierte, zu einer Standortbestimmung zeitgenössischer Architektur und Landschaftsarchitektur. Die IBA Berlin der achtziger Jahre stellte Sanierung und Neubau in der bestehenden Stadt in den Mittelpunkt, die IBA Emscher Park war in den neunziger Jahren der in Bauten sichtbare Motor des Imagewandels im Ruhrgebiet. Auch im Industriellen Gartenreich Dessau – Bitterfeld – Wittenberg in Sachsen-Anhalt gab sich eine Region ein Programm, im Südosten Brandenburgs wird die Bauausstellung „Fürst-Pückler-Land" ebenfalls in einer ehemaligen Industrieregion vorbereitet.

Ein Vorbild für viele dieser Projekte ist Barcelona. Dort wurde zur Vorbereitung auf die Olympischen Spiele 1992 die gestalterische Qualifizierung des öffentlichen Raums zum Schwerpunkt städtebaulicher Politik erhoben. Parks und Plätze entstanden teils neu, teils wurden sie erneuert. Die politische Botschaft einer neuen Offenheit und Öffentlichkeit wurde europaweit mit großem Interesse wahrgenommen. In der Folge haben andere Städte wie Lyon in Frankreich oder Glasgow in Schottland damit begonnen, ihre öffentlichen Räume vorbildlich in Szene zu setzen.

Die Bundesgartenschauen, die in Deutschland seit den fünfziger Jahren im Zwei-Jahres-Rythmus stattfinden, setzten erst spät auf stadtweite Ereignisse und die Formulierung eines eigenen Event-Programms für die jeweils gastgebende Stadt oder Region. Doch inzwischen sind sie als Möglichkeit von programmatischer Stadtentwicklung und Freiraumpolitik bei den Kommunen so beliebt, daß Bewerber um eine Bundesgartenschau bereits für die nächsten fünfzehn Jahre feststehen.

Wenn auch der Name Bundesgartenschau fälschlicherweise eine Beteiligung des Bundes verheißt, so werden diese Veranstaltungen von den jeweiligen Bundesländern in großem Maße gefördert. Anders wäre das ambitionierte, dezentrale Konzept der BUGA Potsdam 2001 nicht zu realisieren gewesen. Es folgt dem niederländischen Beispiel Floriade Zoetermeer 1992, wo eine Gartenschau zum Impuls für die Entwicklung einer neuen Stadt funktionalisiert worden war. Dem Vorbild Potsdam folgen nun weitere Städte. Rostock will mit der Internationalen Gartenschau 2003 zugleich eine neue Warnow-Querung realisieren und die Peripherie der Stadt aufwerten, die BUGA 2005 München soll das Messegelände und den Stadtteil München-Riem qualifizieren und vermarkten, 2007 wird im thüringischen Gera und Ronneburg gar eine Region zum BUGA-Thema, die bisher durch Uran-Abbau ausstrahlte. 2009 wird die mecklenburgische Landeshauptstadt Schwerin ihr Stadtgebiet, den See und die Landschaft in 12 BUGA-Kulissen präsentieren. 2011 sollen in Duisburg Blumen und Bäume in den blauen Himmel über der Ruhr wachsen. Es ist dieser Trend zur Festivalisierung der Stadtentwicklung, der die manchen schon als gestrig geltende Institution Gartenschau mit neuen Inhalten füllt.

In Potsdam war die Ausgangssituation auf vielfältige Weise kompliziert. Denn die Stadt mußte seit 1990 eine neue Identität finden: Im Schatten der nahen Bundeshauptstadt Berlin, zugleich eigenständige Landeshauptstadt Brandenburgs, später wohl eines Bundeslandes Berlin-Brandenburg. Zu der Identitätssuche kam die schwierige ökonomische Lage; die leeren Stadtkassen rückten während der Jahre der BUGA-Planung immer deutlicher in den Mittelpunkt der Politik. Dennoch ließen sich die Lösungen der anstehenden Probleme nicht hinausschieben. Schließlich eröffnete der Abzug der sowjetischen Militärs bis 1994 nicht nur erhebliche Chancen, sondern forderte im Umkehrschluß auch Handlungsbereitschaft angesichts der weißen Flecken im Stadtplan. Und auch die Innenstadt wies sanierungsbedürftige Bausubstanz aus wie das Holländische Viertel, auf das der wachsende Touristenstrom mit viel Neugierde schaut. Substanz sanieren, Tradition bewahren und zugleich neue Ziele definieren, Neues schaffen, vor dieser Quadratur der Herausforderungen stand und steht Potsdam. Die Bundesgartenschau hat in dieser Hinsicht einiges zur Diskussion gestellt.

Fahrrad fahren und Skaten sind sportliche und spielerische Nutzungen, die in den historischen Anlagen wie dem Park Sanssouci oder dem Neuen Garten verboten sind. Der Planung für den neuen Park im Bornstedter Feld ging daher das Motto voran, einen respektablen Volkspark der Gegenwart für Potsdam zu schaffen.

Auf dem einst vom Militär eingenommenen Bornstedter Feld erweitert sich die Stadt erstmals nach Norden. Dafür wurde zu Beginn der neunziger Jahre eine eigene, städtisch getragene Entwicklungsgesellschaft gegründet, die als Initial des Städtebaus einen neuen Park etablierte.

Das städtebauliche Umfeld wird in vier Quartieren teils parallel zum Park, teils auch erst nach der Bundesgartenschau 2001 entwickelt. Die Stadterweiterung Potsdams wird nicht nur neue Wohnangebote machen – geplant sind ca. 7.500 Wohnungen –, sondern auch Gewerbe- und Dienstleistungsstandorte anbieten. Die besondere Herausforderung besteht in der Umwandlung ehemaliger Kasernenkomplexe in solche gemischt genutzten Areale. Ziel für das gesamte Bornstedter Feld ist die integrierte Stadtentwicklung. Auf diesem Weg hat die Städtebauplanung in den letzten Jahren die ursprünglichen Konzepte, verdichtetes Wohnen in Innenstadtnähe anzubieten, sukzessive weiterentwickelt. Inzwischen finden sich in den geplanten Quartieren auch nachgefragte Reihenhäuser und Stadtvillen.

Besonders auf die qualitätvolle Übereinstimmung von Gestaltung und Funktion in Referenz zum jeweiligen Standort wurde vom Entwicklungsträger Bornstedter Feld viel Wert gelegt. Eine große Zahl an Wettbewerben und Auswahlverfahren haben einige vorbildliche Lösungen zeitgemäßer Architektur hervorgebracht, wie etwa der inzwischen realisierte, äußerst skulptural wirkende Wohnungsbau an der Pappelallee auf dem Gelände des ehemaligen Lazaretts, entworfen von dem Berliner Architekten Benedict Tonon, oder das „Tor zum Park", ein städtebaulich prägnanter Entwurf des Hamburger Architekten Bernhard Winking. Darüber hinaus initiierte die Entwicklungsgesellschaft Workshops zu kostensparendem Wohnungsbau und versuchte, angesichts der zunehmend reduzierten öffentlichen Förderung neue Investorenmodelle zu entwickeln. Die privaten Bauträger, die im Rahmen der städtebaulichen Konzeption des Entwicklungsträgers Bornstedter Feld selbst zu Anbietern von Gebäuden oder Siedlungen werden, setzen meist auf das Image Potsdams als Stadt der Gärten und Parks. Entsprechend wichtig ist für ihre Bau- und Vermarktungskonzepte daher der neue Park im Bornstedter Feld.

Zur Akzeptanz der Bundesgartenschau 2001, mit der erhebliche planerische Anstrengungen in Potsdam ausgelöst wurden, hat man sich nicht allein auf einen neuen Park verlassen. Aufgrund vielfacher Erfahrungen in anderen Städten und Regionen wuchs im Potsdam der neunziger Jahre die Überzeugung, den Prozeß der Veränderung selbst ebenfalls zu thematisieren.

Städtebauliche und landschaftsarchitektonische Antworten wurden in allen vier BUGA-Kulissen gesucht. Potsdam stellt sich mit der Bundesgartenschau 2001 seiner Geschichte als Stadt der Gartenkunst. In einer Stadt, in der wesentliche Abschnitte der Gartenkunstgeschichte bis heute so dominant sichtbar sind und durch die UNESCO zum Weltkulturerbe erklärt wurden, die aber dennoch nicht Museum, sondern lebendige Stadt ist, muß die Diskussion um Gegenwart und Zukunft der Landschaftsarchitektur eine wesentliche Rolle spielen.

Es sind die als Event City international diskutierten Konzepte der Stadt- und Landschaftsentwicklung, die heute den Gartenschauen zu neuer Aufmerksamkeit verhelfen. Gartenkunst wird zur Beförderung der Stadtentwicklung gezielt eingesetzt. Selbst ein führendes deutsches Nachrichtenmagazin definierte im Jahresrückblick 2000 die „Gartenkunst als Publikumsrenner". Offen bleibt freilich die Frage, ob die gegenwärtige Aufmerksamkeit für die Landschaftsarchitektur ein kurzfristiger Trend ist, oder ob den Gärten und Parks die notwendige Zeit zum Wachsen und Reifen bleibt. Schon heute ist deutlich, daß die Anlage eines neuen Parks für die Kommunen auch eine große Anstrengung

bedeutet. Die langfristige Pflege und Unterhaltung des Neugeschaffenen ist an die Frage gekoppelt, ob diese privatwirtschaftlich oder aus öffentlichen Kassen finanziert werden kann. Das Leitbild des „aktivierenden Staates", das überall bemüht wird und den Rückzug der öffentlichen Hand aus vielen angestammten Verantwortungsbereichen umschreibt, ist gerade für den öffentlichen Raum ein problematisches. Denn eine einmal durch ein Event ausgelöste Entwicklung eines Ortes bedarf der dauerhaften Unterstützung. Fällt diese weg, muß auch der Ort in seiner Event-Funktion und -Gestalt in Frage gestellt werden. Die Landschaftsarchitektur der Gegenwart, die Gartenkunst 2001, wird am Beispiel Potsdams lernen müssen, kurzfristige Chancen und Moden mit langfristig tragbaren Konzepten zu einem Kunstwerk der Entwicklung und Entspannung zu verbinden. Denn Potsdam hat durch seine vorausschauende und innovative Bundesgartenschau 2001 den beschriebenen Trend mitbegründet.

Horticultural Show –
Performance and potential

The electors, kings and emperors have long since left Potsdam. Many critics would have us believe that these rulers took any aspirations to create beautiful gardens and fine architecture away with them. In fact, democratic states and cities are usually aware of their duty to public spaces and urban design, but nowadays they tend to use the opportunities provided by an overarching festival when they want to make financial and political efforts on the former monarchical scale.

Events of this kind are not restricted to landscape architecture and horticulture. We have World Fairs and the Olympic Games, and also building exhibitions like Interbau 1957 in Berlin, which used the Hansaviertel to demonstrate West Berlin's claim for the future as a defining location for contemporary architecture and landscape architecture. The International Building Exhibition Berlin in the eighties focused on redevelopment and new building in the existing city, and the International Building Exhibition Emscher Park in the nineties was the motor and built manifestation of the Ruhr's change of image. Another region also created a programme for itself in the Industrielles Gartenreich of Dessau – Bitterfeld – Wittenberg in Saxony-Anhalt, and in southeast Brandenburg the Fürst-Pückler-Land Building Exhibition is also being prepared in a former industrial area.

Many of these projects are modelled on Barcelona, where raising the design quality of public space became the key feature of urban development policy during the preparations for the Olympic Games in 1992. Some new parks and squares were created, some were renovated. The political message of new openness and public quality was received with great interest all over Europe. Subsequently, other cities like Lyon in France or Glasgow in Scotland have started to turn their public spaces into models of urban design.

The National Horticultural Show that has taken place every two years in Germany since the fifties came late to the idea of events involving the whole town or city and to formulating a programme of events for the host city or region. But in the meantime they have become so popular with local authorities as a way of triggering an urban development programme and open space policy that applications are in place for the next fifteen years.

The name National Horticultural Show wrongly implies funding by central government; in fact these events are largely financed by the Land in which the show takes place. The ambitious, decentralized concept could not have been realized in any other way; it follows the Dutch example of the Floriade Zoetermeer 1992, where a horticultural show was used to give impetus to the development of a new town. Other towns and cities are now following Potsdam's example. Rostock will be using the International Horticultural Show in 2003 as a means of building a new Warnow river crossing and enhancing the periphery of the city; BUGA 2005 in Munich is intended to enhance and market the Exhibition Centre and the Riem district; in 2007 a whole region formerly polluted by uranium radiation will be the BUGA theme in Gera and Ronneburg in Thuringia. In 2009 Schwerin, the capital of Mecklenburg, will present the town, the lake and the countryside in 12 settings. In 2011 flowers and trees are to grow into the blue skies over the river Ruhr in Duisburg. It is this trend towards making a festival of urban development that has given a new meaning to the Horticultural Show as an institution that many people thought had had its day.

In Potsdam the starting-point was complicated for a number of reasons. The town had had to find a new identity since 1990: it was in the shadow of the nearby national capital, Berlin, at the same time itself capital of Brandenburg, then possibly later of a Land called Berlin-Brandenburg. As well as searching for a new identity, Potsdam was in a difficult economic situation; empty municipal coffers were shifting more and more clearly into the centre of politics during the years in which the National Horticultural Show was being planned. Nevertheless, the problems Potsdam faced had to be solved. Finally the withdrawal of the Soviet forces, completed by 1994, not only provided considerable opportunities, but conversely also required greater commitment in terms of the white spaces on the town plan. And the town centre also had building stock that was in need of refurbishment, like the Holländisches Viertel, for example, which the growing stream of tourists was looking at with a great deal of curiosity. Refurbishing existing building stock, maintaining traditions and at the same time defining new targets, creating new things: Potsdam faced and still faces having to square this circle of problems. The National Horticultural Show has raised various issues in this respect.

Cycling and skateboarding are sports and games that are

forbidden in historical areas like the Sanssouci park or the Neuer Garten. So planning for the new Park in the Bornstedter Feld worked on the basis of creating a respectable contemporary people's park for Potsdam.

The city is expanding northwards for the first time in the Bornstedter Feld, which used to be occupied by the army. A specific, municipally funded development company was set up in the early nineties, and it settled on a park as the first urban development phase.

The urban surroundings will be developed in four districts, partly at the same time as the park, and partly after the 2001 National Horticultural Show. Potsdam's expansion will not just provide new housing – approximately 7,500 dwellings are planned –, but will also offer locations for commerce and services. The particular challenge lies in transforming former barracks into areas for mixed use of this kind. The aim for the whole of the Bornstedter Feld is integrated urban development. This is how urban planning in recent years has successively refined the original concepts of offering high-density housing close to the town centre. Terraced and town houses are much in demand, and these are also to be found in the new districts.

The Bornstedter Feld developers were particularly concerned that design and function should harmonize and be of high quality in relation to each specific site. A large number of competitions and selection procedures produced some model solutions in terms of contemporary architecture, like for example the residential building on Pappelallee, highly sculptural in its appearance, that has been built on the site of the former military hospital, designed by the Berlin architect Benedict Tonon, or the "Gate to the Park", a succinct piece of urban design by the Hamburg architect Bernhard Winking. As well as this, the development company set up workshops for cost-saving housing construction and establish new investors' incentive schemes given the steady reduction of public funding. Private building firms, who are themselves offering buildings or housing estates to fit in with the Bornstedter Feld's developers' concept, usually base themselves on the image of Potsdam as a town of gardens and parks. Thus the new Park in the Bornstedter Feld is correspondingly important for their building and marketing concepts.

The National Horticultural Show 2001 has triggered a great deal of exertion in planning in Potsdam: the town has not relied only on a new park to make it attractive. Having considered a wide variety of experiences in other cities and regions, people in Potsdam became increasingly convinced in the early nineties that the process of change itself should be made a theme.

Responses in terms of urban design and landscape architecture were sought in all four BUGA settings. Here Potsdam is facing up to its reputation as the city of garden history, a city in which substantial chapters of horticultural history still dominate the scene, and have been declared World Heritage Sites by UNESCO. Yet it is not a museum, but a living entity, and discussion about the present and future of landscape architecture plays a key role in all the planning processes.

Urban and landscape development concepts which are being discussed internationally as Event City are drawing increasing attention to the Horticultural Shows. Garden Art is being deliberately used to promote urban development. Even a leading German news magazine cited "garden art as a best-seller with the public" in its retrospective on the year 2000. And yet the question remains open of whether current interest in landscape architecture is merely a short-term trend or whether the gardens and parks will be given sufficient time to grow and mature. It is clear that establishing a new park involves a great deal of effort by local authorities. Long-term planning and maintenance of what has been created is linked with the question of whether this can be financed privately or publicly. The model of the "activating state" that is being aspired to everywhere indicates that public funding is being withdrawn from many of its customary areas of responsibility. This is particularly problematical when it affects public spaces: a development that has been triggered by a one-off event in a certain place in fact needs continuing support. If this disappears, then the venue's function and form in relation to the event is called into question. Contemporary landscape architecture – Garden Art 2001 – will have to learn from Potsdam's example and combine short-term opportunities and fashions with concepts that are sustainable in the long term, in order to create works of art for leisure and recreation. Potsdam has helped to establish this trend with its visionary and innovative National Horticultural Show 2001.

1 Ob bei den Wasserspielen in den Wällen, ob auf den Spielgeräten im Waldpark, die Kinder können in den eigens für sie gestalteten Bereichen ihrem Bewegungsdrang folgen.

Children can be active to their hearts' content on the water features in the "ramparts" or on the play apparatus in the Wooded Park, specially designed for them.

2 Der einsame, verwunschene Thron im Nuthepark wird von den Kindern eingenommen.

The lonely, enchanted throne in the Nuthepark has been adopted by children.

2

❶ Die vielfältig gestalteten Wälle sind die letzten Zeugen der über 200 Jahre währenden militärischen Vergangenheit.

The varied "ramparts" are the last evidence of a military past going back over 200 years.

❷ An den Rändern des Parks erinnern große Portraits daran, daß bis vor einigen Jahren russische Soldaten die einzigen Bewohner des Gebietes waren. Fotoinstallation von Frank Gaudlitz, Potsdam.

Large portraits at the edges of the park remind us that until a few years ago Russian soldiers were the only people who lived in this area. Photo installation by Frank Gaudlitz, Potsdam.

❷

National Horticultural Show Potsdam 2001 Projects, Designers, Competition Results

Kulisse Park im Bornstedter Feld
Park in the Bornstedter Feld venue

Entwicklungsträger Bornstedter Feld GmbH
Geschäftsführer | Managing director:
Volker Härtig
Koordination | Coordination:
Diethild Kornhardt

Bundesgartenschau Potsdam 2001 GmbH
Geschäftsführer | Managing director:
Jochen Sandner

Park im Bornstedter Feld
Park in the Bornstedter Feld

Landschaftsplanerisch-Städtebaulicher Ideenwettbewerb mit vorgeschaltetem Bewerbungs-
verfahren | Landscape planning and urban
development ideas competition with preliminary
application procedure
3 / 1997

1. Preis | 1st prize
Latz + Partner Landschaftsarchitekten;
Kranzberg, Peter Latz
Jourda & Perraudin Architectes; Lyon / Hegger –
Hegger – Schleiff HHS Planer + Architekten;
Kassel

2. Preis | 2nd prize
Gerwin Engel, Jens Henningsen
Büro Henningsen und Partner; Berlin
Landschaftsarchitekten | Landscape architects
Frank Dörken, Volker Heise; Berlin
Architekten | Architects

3. Preis | 3rd prize
AG Freiraum Jochen Dittus,
Andreas Böhringer; Freiburg
Landschaftsarchitekten | Landscape architects
Hermann Binkert, Thomas Melder; Freiburg
Architekten | Architects

4. Preis | 4th prize
Büro Stötzer; Sindelfingen/Berlin
Landschaftsarchitekten | Landscape architects
Ackermann + Raff; Tübingen
Architekten | Architects

5. Preis | 5th prize
I. Schmitz, Thomas Wollny; Berlin
Landschaftsarchitekten | Landscape architects
Blase + Kapici; Berlin
Architekten | Architects

1. Ankauf | 1st mention
Luz + Partner; Stuttgart
Landschaftsarchitekten | Landscape architects
Behnisch, Behnisch + Partner; Stuttgart
Architekten | Architects

2. Ankauf | 2nd mention
Büro Louafi; Berlin Kamel Louafi
Landschaftsarchitekten | Landscape architects
Reimar Herbst, Martin Lang; Berlin
Architekten | Architects

3. Ankauf | 3rd mention
Winy Maas, Büro MVRDV; Rotterdam
Hemprich + Tophof; Berlin
Architekten | Architects

4. Ankauf | 4th mention
L.A.U.B. GmbH; Potsdam
Landschaftsarchitekten | Landscape architects
COOPERA; Dresden
Architekten | Architects

Entwurf und Realisierung der Teil-
bereiche im „Park im Bornstedter Feld"
Design and realization for sections of
the "Park in the Bornstedter Feld"

GROSSER WIESENPARK, KLEINER WIESENPARK
LARGE AND SMALL MEADOW PARKS
Latz + Partner Landschaftsarchitekten;
Kranzberg, Peter Latz

GROSSER WIESENPARK – PARKFENSTER
LARGE MEADOW PARK – PARK WINDOW
Büro Röntz; Berlin
Landschaftsarchitektin | Landscape architect

GROSSER WIESENPARK – PARKFINGER
LARGE MEADOW PARK – PARK FINGER
Latz + Partner Landschaftsarchitekten;
Kranzberg

GROSSER WIESENPARK – WASSERSPIELPLATZ
LARGE MEADOW PARK – WATER PLAYGROUND
Andrea Schirmer; Berlin
Landschaftsarchitektin | Landscape architect

CAFÉ AM SPIELWALL
CAFÉ AT THE PLAY RAMPART
Gnädinger Architekten, Berlin

„IN DEN WÄLLEN" MIT VISUR
"WITHIN THE RAMPARTS" WITH VISUR
Sommerlad Haase Kuhli Landschaftsarchitekten;
Gießen, Potsdam

PARKDACH | ROOF
Dietrich, Fritzen, Löf; Köln
Architekten | Architects

REMISENPARK | SHELTER PARK
Planungsgemeinschaft Remisenpark; Freiburg
AG Freiraum, Pit Müller
Landschaftsarchitekten | Landscape architects

WALDPARK | WOODED PARK
Entwurf | Design:
Bureau B + B; Amsterdam
Landschaftsarchitekten | Landscape architects
Realisierung, Bauleitung | Realization, site
management:
Thomas Dietrich; Berlin in Zusammenarbeit mit |
in cooperation with Bureau B+B

„TERMINALS" IM WALDPARK
"TERMINALS" AT WOODED PARK
Boss & Frey Architekten; Berlin in Zusammen-
arbeit mit | in cooperation with Bureau B+B

Temporäre Gartenanlagen
Temporary Gardens

TEMPORÄRE AUSSTELLUNGSFLÄCHEN (GRUNDSTRUKTUR), GARTENSITUATIONEN
TEMPORARY EXHIBITION AREAS (BASIC STRUCTURE), GARDEN SITUATIONS
Burger + Tischer; München, Berlin
Landschaftsarchitekten | Landscape architects

GARTENSITUATIONEN, GÄRTEN DER DEKADEN
GARDEN SITUATIONS, DECADE GARDENS
Isterling und Partner; Hamburg
Landschaftsarchitekten | Landscape architects

ROSENBAND, GEHÖLZBILDER UND RHODODENDRONHAIN | COLLAR OF ROSES, COPSE SCENES AND RHODODENDRON GROVE
Bruno Leipacher; Wuppertal
Landschaftsarchitekt | Landscape architect
Kirk + Specht; Berlin
Landschaftsarchitekten | Landscape architects

PYRAMIDENGÄRTEN, PRACHTSTAUDEN, STAUDENBÜHNEN, ERNST-PAGELSSORTIMENTSGARTEN | PYRAMID GARDENS, MAGNIFICIENT HERBACEOUS PLANTS, HERBACEOUS STAGES, ERNST PAGELS ASSORTMENT GARDEN
Christine Orel; Aurachtal
Landschaftsarchitektin | Landscape architect
Christian Meyer; Berlin
Garten- und Landschaftsplaner | Garden and landscape planner

WECHSELFLOR UND EINGANGSBEREICHE
BEDDING PLANTS AND ENTRANCE AREAS
Heinz H. Eckebrecht; Kelkheim
Landschaftsarchitekt | Landscape architect

GRABBEPFLANZUNG UND GRABMAL, GASTRONOMIESTANDORTE, GESUNDHEITSGARTEN, NATURGARTEN, KLEINGÄRTEN
MONUMENT AND GRAVE PLANTING, CATERING SITES, HEALTH GARDEN, NATURAL GARDEN, ALLOTMENTS
Achim Röthig; Haan
Garten- und Landschaftsarchitekt | Garden and landscape architect

GRABBEPFLANZUNG UND GRABMAL, GASTRONOMIESTANDORTE, GÄRTNER- UND BAUERNMARKT | MONUMENT AND GRAVE PLANTING, CATERING SITES, GARDENER AND FARMERMARKET
Wittling & Benninghoff; Berlin
Landschaftsarchitekten | Landscape architects

GESUNDHEITSGARTEN, NATURGARTEN, KLEINGÄRTEN | HEALTH GARDEN, NATURAL GARDEN, ALLOTMENTS
Förder und Demmer; Essen
Landschaftsarchitekten | Landscape architects

PFLANZBAR | PLANT BAR
Saara Hanke, Marek Jahnke; Berlin
Studenten der TU Berlin | Students of Berlin Technical University

LEHRBAUSTELLE BGL | BGL TEACHING SITE
Susanne Pfaffenstiel, Florian Otto; Berlin, München
Studenten der TU Berlin und TU München | Students of Berlin Technical University and Munich Technical University

Wettbewerb „Kunst im Park", Park im Bornstedter Feld
"Art in the Park" competition, Park in the Bornstedter Feld
Ideen- und Realisierungswettbewerb für Künstler und Landschaftsarchitekten mit vorgeschaltetem Auswahlverfahren | Ideas and building competition for artists and landscape architects with preselection procedure
1998

Realisiert wurden | Built projects

Annette Wehrmann; Hamburg: „DER TURM"

Künstlergruppe inges idee; Berlin: „BASKETBALLFELD"

Andreas Siekmann; Berlin: „HIER BAUT DIE FIRMA PETIT À PETIT"

Fritz Balthaus; Berlin: „K"

Künstlergruppe BergWerk; Potsdam: „CAMOFIELDS – Volle Deckung"

Igor Sacharow-Ross; Köln: „DER ZAUN"

Temporäre Architektur, Möblierung
Temporary architecture, furniture

Kassenpavillons | Ticket pavilions
Prof. Ludger Brands, Daniela Hinz
Fachhochschule Potsdam | Potsdam College

Wettbewerb „Möblierung, Ausstattung"
"Furniture and Furnishings" competition
1 / 2000

1. Rang | 1st prize
Büro Botsch; Berlin
Architekten | Architects

2. Rang | 2nd prize
Monopol +, Lutz Köbele, Martin Rissler; Berlin
mit | with Planergemeinschaft Dubach Kohlbrenner; Berlin

3. Rang | 3rd prize
[kunst + technik] Martin Janekovic, Jonathan Garnham, Rainer Hartl, Uwe Rieger, Helle Schröder; Berlin
Architekten | Architects

Ankauf | Mention
n/p/k Industrial Design; Leiden NL

Realisierung | Realization
Realisiert wurde die im Wettbewerb zur Berücksichtigung empfohlene Bank der Architekten [kunst + technik] | The bench by [kunst + technik] Architekten was selected for realization

Informations- und Leitsystem | Information and circulation system
Rambow + van den Sand; Berlin

Park im Bornstedter Feld: Neubau von Brücken | Park in the Bornstedter Feld: New Bridges
Beschränkter Realisierungswettbewerb für Architekten und Ingenieure mit vorgeschaltetem Bewerberverfahren | Building competition by invitation for architects and engineers with preliminary application procedure
11 / 1998

1. Preis und Realisierung | 1st prize
and realization
Prof. Dietrich, Fritzen, Löf; Köln
Ingenieurbüro Horz + Ladewig; Köln

2. Preis | 2nd prize
Werkfabrik; Berlin
Ingenieurgesellschaft für Tragwerksplanung
mbH Dipl.-Ing. Herbert Pape; Berlin

3. Preis | 3rd prize
Gerhard Münster; Berlin
IPP Prof. Dr.-Ing. Polonyi + Partner GmbH; Köln

Park im Bornstedter Feld – Rahmenplanung | Park in the the Bornstedter Feld – Overall planning

Gruppe F; Berlin
Büro für Landschaftsentwicklung und Freiraumgestaltung

Park im Bornstedter Feld – Koordination und Projektsteuerung der Realisierung | Park in the Bornstedter Feld – Coordination and supervision of realization

Büro Landschaft Planen & Bauen; Berlin
IRWAG. Beratende Ingenieure; Berlin

Biosphäre Potsdam
Potsdam Biosphere

Realisierungswettbewerb mit vorgeschaltetem
Auswahlverfahren | Building competition with
pre-selection procedure
5 / 1999

1. Preis und Realisierung | 1st prize
and realization
Barkow Leibinger Architekten; Berlin
Frank Barkow, Regine Leibinger
Landschaftsarchitektur | Landscape architecture:
Büro Kiefer; Berlin

2. Preis | 2nd prize
Hascher + Jehle Architekten und Ingenieure;
Berlin
Landschaftsarchitektur | Landscape architecture:
ST raum a.; Berlin

Ankauf | Mention
Rüdiger Kramm in Kramm + Strigl; Darmstadt

Ankauf | Mention
Jürgen Franke, Frank Zimmermann; Cottbus
Landschaftsarchitektur | Landscape architecture:
H. M. Eckebrecht; Cottbus

Ankauf | Mention
Architekten Schweger + Partner; Hannover
Landschaftsarchitektur | Landscape architecture:
Diekmann; Hannover

REALISIERUNG DER AUSSENANLAGEN ZUR BIOSPHÄRE POTSDAM | REALIZATION OF OPEN SPACES FOR THE POTSDAM BIOSPHERE
Büro Kiefer; Berlin
Landschaftsarchitekten | Landscape architects

REALISIERUNG DER PFLANZUNGEN ZUR ERLEBNISLANDSCHAFT IN DER BIOSPHÄRE | REALIZATION OF PLANTING FOR ADVENTURE AREA IN THE BIOSPHERE
Martin Diekmann, Hannover
Landschaftsarchitekt | Landscape architect

Bornstedter Feld – Städtebau und Architektur | Bornstedter Feld – Urban Design and Architecture

KASERNE PAPPELALLEE, WOHNGEBIET AM SCHRAGEN
Städtebaulicher Wettbewerb |
Urban development competition
10 / 1994

1. Preis | 1st prize
Becher + Rottkamp; Berlin
Architekten | Architects
Thomanek + Duquesnoy
Landschaftsarchitekten | Landscape architects

2. Preis | 2nd prize
Peter Scheck für Thalen Consult; Berlin
Architekt | Architect
Andreas Riker, Freiraumplanung

3. Preis | 3rd prize
Georg-P. Mügge; Berlin
Architekt | Architect
Bernhardt Palluch, Ökologie; Berlin

4. Preis | 4th prize
Klaus P. Springer; Berlin
Architekt | Architect
Engel und Sauer; Berlin
Landschaftsarchitekten | Landscape architects

5. Preis | 5th prize
Christian Kennerknecht; Berlin
Architekt | Architect
Michael Palm; Weinheim
Landschaftsarchitekt | Landscape architect

Ankauf | Mention
Hufnagel Pütz Rafaelian; Berlin
Architekten | Architects
Gabriele Lanzrath
Landschaftsarchitektin | Landscape architect

Ankauf | Mention
Hemprich + Tophof; Berlin
Architekten | Architects
Büro Kiefer; Berlin
Landschaftsarchitekten | Landscape architects

NEUBEBAUUNG AM LAZARETT | NEW BUILDINGS AT LAZARETT
Gutachterverfahren | Expert report procedure
1995

1. Preis und Realisierung | 1st prize
and realisation
Prof. Benedict Tonon; Berlin
Architekt | Architect

KASERNE KIRSCHALLEE
KIRSCHALLEE BARRACKS
Gutachterverfahren | Expert report procedure
1995

1. Preis | 1st prize
Büro plus +; Neckartenzlingen
Architekten | Architects

2. Preis | 2nd prize
Faskel + Becher; Berlin
und | and Kaleschke; Duisburg
Architekten | Architects

3. Preis | 3rd prize
Büro Eichstädt / Bühlhoff; Berlin mit | with Büro
Prof. Hofstadt & Schneider, Büro Kohl & Kohl
Architekten | Architects

STÄDTEBAULICHE NEUORDNUNG KASERNE
KIRSCHALLEE | URBAN DEVELOPMENT
KIRSCHALLEE BARRACKS
Büro plus +; Neckartenzlingen und | and
Hübner/Blanke/Forster
Architekten | Architects

Abschnitt Wohnen am Park und Schulblock
Living at park and school area
Arge Büros Eichstädt / Bühlhoff; Berlin und | and
Faskel + Becker; Berlin
Architekten | Architects

ARCHITEKTEN- UND INVESTOREN-AUSWAHL-
VERFAHREN „SÜDLICHE GARTENSTADT KIRSCH-
ALLEE" | ARCHITECTS' AND INVESTORS' SELEC-
TION PROCEDURE "KIRSCHALLEE GARDEN
TOWN SOUTH"
3 / 1998

BOTAG (Baufeld | Building area WA 4)
with | mit R. Oefelein; Berlin
Architekten | Architects

Dormagener Wohnungsbau (Baufeld | Building
area WA 2,3) with | mit Heider, Kürten,
Langwagen; Köln
Architekten | Architects

SPORTPLATZ QUARTIER KASERNE KIRSCHALLEE
KIRSCHALLEE BARRACKS AREA SPORTSGROUND
Büro Henningsen und Partner; Berlin
Landschaftsarchitekten | Landscape architects

KOSTENSPARENDER WOHNUNGSBAU KASERNE
PAPPELALLEE | LOW-COST HOUSING
PAPPELALLEE BARRACKS
Gutachterverfahren | Expert report procedure
12 / 1996

Ausgewählte Entwürfe | Selected designs
Astoc / Prof. Kees Christiaanse
Springer, Fink + Jocher, Mügge

STÄDTEBAULICHES KONZEPT KASERNE
PAPPELALLEE | URBAN DEVELOPMENT CON-
CEPT PAPPELALLEE BARRACKS
6 / 2000

Ausgewähltes Konzept | Selected concept
Günther F. Großmann; Berlin
Architekt | Architect

Neubau „Das Tor zum Park"
"Gateway to the Park" building
Ideen- und Realisierungswettbewerb für
Architekten | Ideas and building competition for
architects
10 / 1999

1. Preis und Realisierung | 1st prize
and realization
Bernhard Winking Architekten
mit | with Martin Floh, arbos, Peter Köster
Landschaftsarchitektur | Landscape architecture;
Hamburg/Berlin

2. Preis | 2nd prize
Architekten Lahr-Eigen & Partner; Potsdam
Peter Danisch, Georg Lahr-Eigen, Uwe Salzl

3. Preis | 3rd prize
Carola Schäfers; Berlin
Architektin | Architect
Büro Kiefer; Berlin
Landschaftsarchitekten | Landscape architects

PLATZ AM „TOR ZUM PARK"
SQUARE AT "GATEWAY TO THE PARK"
Levin Monsigny; Berlin
Landschaftsarchitekten | Landscape architects

HANDWERKERHOF „ROTE KASERNE OST"
CRAFT YARD "RED BARRACKS EAST"
Gutachterverfahren | Expert report procedure
10 / 1999

1. Preis | 1st prize
Sroka Architekten; Berlin

2. Preis | 2nd prize
Autzen & Reimers; Berlin
Architekten | Architects

3. Preis | 3rd prize
Eric van Geisten, Georg Marfels; Potsdam
Architekten | Architects
Raul van Geisten; Potsdam
Garten- und Landschaftsplanung | Garden and
landscape planning

ENTWICKLUNGSGEBIET AM JUNGFERNSEE
DEVELOPMENT AREA AT JUNGFERNSEE
Städtebauliches und landschaftsplanerisches
Gutachterverfahren | Urban development and
landscape planning expert report procedure
1 / 2001

1. Preis | 1st prize
Ortner & Ortner Baukunst; Berlin
Architekten | Architects
Hannelore Kossel; Berlin
Landschaftsarchitektin | Landscape architect

2. Preis | 2nd prize
Steidle & Partner, Berlin
Architekten | Architects
Stefan Tischer; Berlin
Landschaftsarchitekt | Landscape architect

3. Preis | 3rd prize
Kahlfeld Architekten; Berlin
Kamel Louafi; Berlin
Landschaftsarchitekt | Landscape architect

Kulisse Bornstedter Feldflur
Bornstedt Meadowland venue

Wettbewerb Bornstedter Feldflur
Bornstedt Meadowland competition
Ideen- und Realisierungswettbewerb für
Künstler, Landschaftsarchitekten und Agraringe-
nieure mit vorgeschaltetem Auswahlverfahren|
Ideas and building competition for artists, landscape architects and agricultural engineers with
pre-selection procedure
2 – 7 / 1998
nicht realisiert | not realized

1. Preis | 1st prize
Rotzler Krebs Partner; Zürich,
Stefan Rotzler
Landschaftsarchitekt | Landscape architect
Otmar Sattel; Berlin
Künstler | Artist
Hermann Giebelhausen; Berlin
Agraringenieur | Agricultural engineer

2. Preis | 2nd prize
West 8 Landschaftsarchitekten; Rotterdam,
Adriaan Geuze
Landschaftsarchitekt | Landscape architect
Inge Mahn; Berlin
Künstlerin | Artist
Wilfried Hübner; Berlin
Agraringenieur | Agricultural engineer

3. Preis | 3rd prize
ST raum a.; Berlin,
Stefan Jäckel, Tobias Micke
Landschaftsarchitekten | Landscape architects
Francis Zeischegg; Berlin
Künstlerin | Artist
Anette Wackerhagen; Berlin
Agraringenieurin | Agricultural engineer

1. Sonderpreis | 1st special prize
Büro Sprenger; Berlin
Annette Sprenger, Daniel Sprenger
Landschaftsarchitekten | Landscape architects
Jörg Schlinke, Künstlergruppe BergWerk;
Potsdam,
Künstler | Artists
Barthelmes; Berlin
Agraringenieur | Agricultural engineer

2. Sonderpreis | 2nd special prize
Büro Geskes; Berlin, Christoph Geskes
Landschaftsarchitekt | Landscape architect

Simone Mangos; Berlin
Künstlerin | Artist
Baumecker; Berlin
Agraringenieur | Agricultural engineer

3. Sonderpreis | 3rd special prize
Büro Röntz; Berlin, Ariane Röntz
Landschafts-architektin | Landscape architect
Edward A. Dormer; Potsdam
Künstler | Artist
Cord Petermann, Tanja Runge; Berlin
Agraringenieure | Agricultural engineers

Flurneuordnungsverfahren Bornim-
Bornstedter Feldflur | Reorganization of
the Bornim-Bornstedt Meadowland
Rekonstruktion der historischen Kulturlandschaft
Reconstruction of the historical cultural landscape

Brandenburgisches Ministerium für Landwirtschaft, Umweltschutz und Raumordnung, Amt
für Flurneuordnung und ländliche Entwicklung

Modellkleingartenanlage Kirschallee
Kirschallee model allotments
Vertiefungsverfahren 1999 zu dem 1998 durchge-
führten Wettbewerb „Bornstedter Feldflur"
Advanced work in 1999 on the "Bornstedt
Meadowland" competition of 1998

Büro Kiefer; Berlin
Landschaftsarchitekten | Landscape architects

**LAUBEN IN DER MODELLKLEINGARTENANLAGE
KIRSCHALLEE | SUMMER-HOUSES IN KIRSCH-
ALLEE MODEL ALLOTMENTS**
Architekten- und Hersteller-Auswahlverfahren
Architects' and producers' selection procedure
11 / 2000

Preisträger | Winner
Jörg Joppien; Berlin
Architekt | Architect

Gartendenkmalpflegerische Wiederher-
stellung des Karl-Foerster-Gartens,
Bornim | Reconstruction in terms of
historical garden preservation of the
Karl-Foerster-Garten, Bornim
Martin Heisig, Freie Planungsgruppe Berlin
Landschaftsarchitekt | Landscape architect

Kulissen Historische Innenstadt /
Orte am Fluss
Historic City Centre / Riverside
venues

Sanierungsträger Potsdam-Gesellschaft für
behutsame Stadterneuerung mbH, Potsdam
Geschäftsführer | Managing director: Cornelius
van Geisten (bis 1997), Bernd Cronjaeger
Koordination | Coordination: Rose Fisch

Platz der Einheit | Unity Square
Internationaler eingeladener Ideen- und
Realisierungswettbewerb | International ideas
and building competition by invitation
5 / 1997

1. Preis / 1st prize
WES & Partner Landschaftsarchitekten Wehberg,
Eppinger, Schmidke, Schatz, Betz; Hamburg,
Hinnerk Wehberg

2. Preis | 2nd prize
Guido Hager; Zürich
Landschaftsarchitekt | Landscape architect

3. Preis | 3rd prize
EXTERN Garten- und Landschaftsarchitektur
Heinz Kluth, Fritz Prötzmann, Susanne Vollmer;
Potsdam

Lustgarten / Alter Markt
Lustgarten / Old Market
Zweistufiger Ideen- und Realisierungswettbewerb
Two-phase ideas and building competition
7 / 1997

**1. Preis und Realisierung | 1st prize
and realization**
Dietz Joppien Architekten; Berlin/Potsdam
Albert Dietz, Anett-Maud Joppien
Büro freiRaum. Planungsgruppe Stadt Garten
Landschaft; Kiedrich
Barbara Willecke, Lutz Neuschaefer
Landschaftsarchitekten | Landscape architects
mit | with Reinhard Angelis
Architekt | Architect
(Wettbewerb | competition)
Seebauer, Wefers und Partner
Landschaftsarchitekten; Berlin
(Realisierung | realization)

2. Preis | 2nd prize
Thomas Göbel-Groß; Karlsruhe
Henning M. Baumann; Karlsruhe
Landschaftsarchitekten | Landscape architects

3. Preis | 3rd prize
Bernd Meier; Freiburg
Manfred Morlock; Schallstadt

Freundschaftsinsel | Friendship Island
Gartendenkmalpflegerische Analyse und Konzeption der Wiederherstellung | Analysis and concept of restauration in terms of historical garden preservation

TOPOS Landschafts- und Stadtplanung; Berlin
Bettina Bergande, Manfred Schültken

BASSINPLATZ | BASIN SQUARE
Gartendenkmalpflegerische Konzeption | Concept in terms of historical garden preservation

WES & Partner Landschaftsarchitekten Wehberg Eppinger, Schmidke, Schatz, Betz; Hamburg
Hinnerk Wehberg

STADTKANAL | CITY CANAL
Gartendenkmalpflegerische Konzeption | Concept in terms of historical garden preservation
Gruppe Planwerk; Berlin
Siegfried Reibetanz, Klaus Moll

PROMENADE HEGELALLEE
HEGELALLEE PROMENADE
Konzeption und Planung | Concept and planning
Gruppe Planwerk; Berlin
Siegfried Reibetanz, Klaus Moll

FUSSGÄNGERPROMENADE ALTE FAHRT
ALTE FAHRT PEDESTRIAN PROMENADE
Entwurf und Planung | Design and planning
Adam + Partner *Landschaftsarchitekten*; Potsdam

BRÜCKE ÜBER DIE ALTE FAHRT
BRIDGE OVER THE ALTE FAHRT
Entwurf und Planung | Design and planning
Büro Verkehrs- und Ingenieurbau Consult GmbH (VIC), Pust / Dr. Altmann, Potsdam

NUTHEPARK
Entwurf und Realisierung | Design and realization
Fugmann + Janotta Landschaftsarchitekten; Berlin, Martin Janotta, Jörg Bresser

BRÜCKE ÜBER DIE NUTHE
BRIDGE OVER THE NUTHE
Entwurf und Planung | Design and planning
Prof. Siegfried Ast, Obermeyer; Berlin / Potsdam

Bildnachweis | Acknowledgements

Agence Ter; Paris: 25

Barkow Leibinger Architekten; Berlin
46 l., 82 u., 83
Margherita Spiluttini: 84, 85, 86, 87 u.

BUGA Potsdam 2001 GmbH; Ulf Böttcher
16 l., 22 u., 23 u., 42, 43, 44 r. u., 60 l. + r. o., 65 l., 88 l., 101, 117, 120, 120/121, 121 l., 124 u., 125
Gruppe F; Berlin: 56

Büro Kiefer; Berlin: 84 u.

Büro Latz + Partner; Kranzberg
Michael Latz: 24 l.

Dietz Joppien Architekten; Potsdam: 112, 112/113

Entwicklungsträger Bornstedter Feld; Potsdam:
20/21, 22/23
AG Freiraum; Freiburg/Binkert und Melder; Freiburg: 75
B + B; Amsterdam: 73 r.
Büro Röntz; Berlin/Edward A. Dormer: 99 l.
Barkow Leibinger Architekten; Berlin: 82 o.
Frank Gaudlitz; Potsdam: Titel | cover, 16/17, 17 r. o., 18 u., 19, 20 l., 20/21, 21, 22 o., 44/45, 58, 59, 60 r. u., 61, 62, 63, 64, 64/65, 66, 67, 68, 69, 70, 71 u., 134, 136
Christoph Geskes; Berlin: 98
Harald Hirsch; Potsdam: 23 o. + m., 38 u., 44 l., 113 r., 114, 115, 135
Latz + Partner; Kranzberg: 46 r. u., 72, 73 l.
Wini Maas, MVRDV; Rotterdam/Hemprich + Tophof Architekten; Berlin: 74
Levin Monsigny; Berlin: 70/71
Rotzler Krebs Partner; Zürich/Otmar Sattel; Berlin/Hermann Giebelhausen; Berlin: 89, 94, 95
Sprenger Landschaftsarchitekten; Berlin/Jörg Schlinke; Potsdam: 88 r., 99 r.

ST raum a; Berlin/Francis Zeischegg; Berlin/Anette Wackerhagen; Berlin: 97
Sabine Wenzel: Mohnfeld, 46/47
West 8; Rotterdam/Inge Mahn; Berlin/Wilfried Hübner; Berlin: 96

Bet Figueras; Barcelona: 24 o.

GROSS.MAX; Edinburgh: 24 u.

Lutz Hannemann; Potsdam: 17 r. u., 18 o., 57, 87 o., 136/137

Potsdam Museum; Potsdam: 36, 37 o., 100/101
Dörries: 38 o.
Königlich-Preussische Messbildanstalt Berlin: 38/39
Alfred von Loebenstein: 38 u., 123 r.
Städtische Lichtbildstelle Potsdam: 124 o.l.

Sanierungsträger Potsdam; Potsdam:
Dietz Joppien Architekten; Potsdam: 110, 111
Fugmann + Janotta Landschaftsarchitekten; Berlin: 121 r.
Guido Hager: 124 o.r.
TOPOS Landschaftsplanung; Berlin: 116/117, 118, 119
WES & Partner Landschaftsarchitekten Wehberg – Eppinger – Schmidke – Schatz – Betz; Hamburg: 100 u., 123 l.

Stiftung Preußische Schlösser und Gärten Berlin-Brandenburg, Plankammer; Potsdam
40/41, 122

Vignetten | vignettes:
Leitfaden für den Unterricht in der Botanik, bearbeitet von Dr. C. Baenitz, 6. Aufl., Velhagen und Klasing, Bielefeld/Leipzig, 1892 (Titel | cover, 1, 5, 26, 29, 47, 76, 79, 89, 101, 126, 128)